50 WAYS to ENJOY

TURNING

FIFTY

Make the Most of Your Milestone Birthday to Have the Best Year Ever

Ж

Liisa Kyle, Ph.D.

ЖΚ

Contents

Chapter 1

Making the Most of Turning Fifty

Happy Birthday! How are you feeling about your milestone?

If you're happy and excited and looking forward to a wonderful year: Congratulations! Great attitude! This book is designed to help you make the most of turning fifty.

If you're feeling neutral — that's it's just another birthday: Let me ask you this — what if it didn't have to be just another ho-hum year? This book is packed with 50 Ways to make this your best year ever.

If you're full of dread: This book will help you handle it…and turn it into an opportunity to live the life you really want.

If you're in the latter category, I empathize. Over the years, my typical reaction to a milestone birthday has featured depressive symptoms and existential angst, punctuated with self-pity.

I coped with my thirtieth birthday by submerging myself in a vat of Merlot. (Don't judge. I was thirty.)

I dealt with my fortieth by an uncharacteristic, inexplicable shopping splurge. In a fancy art gallery. (It was a very expensive birthday.)

When my fiftieth birthday approached, I had a problem. Much as I wanted an extra special fiftieth birthday celebration…I just couldn't swing it. There were practical constraints to having a big party or taking an exotic trip or any of the traditional ways people honor their milestones.

Rather than get frustrated by the likely mediocrity of my impending birthday, I decided that the day itself was less important than the year ahead. Instead of focusing on having a super special *day* — and risking likely disappointment — I made a commitment to have a terrific *year*.

I asked myself exactly what would make my fiftieth year special for me. What did I love to do? What would I love to do more of?

The first thing that popped into my head was "frolics." I adore going to interesting places and doing fun things. So why not commit to enjoy frolics throughout the twelve months?

As soon as I thought of the concept, I was tickled by the possibilities: Frolics might be mini-adventures or opportunities for creative expression or athletic endeavors. They could be done with others or solo. They could be something completely novel or something I've long adored — favorite hobbies or long forgotten pastimes. I haven't gone horseback riding in a decade, for example. Might it be time to (literally) get back on my horse?

Thinking about the possible options felt great! I decided to focus on enjoying frolics throughout my fiftieth year. As a way of keeping myself on track with my quest, it occurred to me that I should aim to have a certain minimum number of frolics during the year. But how many? The answer was obvious: Fifty.

Thus, I committed to enjoy (at least) fifty frolics during my fiftieth year. To ensure that I follow through, I commenced documenting my efforts in a blog called — you guessed it — "Fifty Frolics."

This blog fostered several things I called my "Fiftieth Projects" i.e. other things I committed to do to make the most of my milestone year. Like reading (at least) fifty books. And trying (at least) fifty new recipes. The point was to identify and do more of what I really love as a way of making the most of my milestone year.

As a result, I did have an amazing fiftieth. MORE IMPORTANTLY, my blog inspired others to make the most of their fiftieth year. Readers wrote to tell me about special events they organized or simple pleasures they re-discovered or once-in-a-lifetime trips they took. I've included their stories throughout this book as inspiration because **different people have very different ideas about how to make the most of turning fifty.** For example, Ellen treated herself to a month's vacation at a beach house — honoring her happiest memories from her youth. Oliver went on safari. Marlene made a point of attending particular concerts that she otherwise would have let pass her by. Kate used her milestone as an excuse to sleep more — and nap whenever she wished — guilt-free.

You can do the same: You can decide to make the most of the next twelve months. To do what you love. To indulge in simple pleasures. To treat yourself to the things you enjoy. To do what's important to you.

Emphasis on **you**. This is not what society says is important. Or what your mom or your boss or your childhood chum believes should be your top priorities. This is the time to be clear and candid about what matters to **you**. After all, if you're going to make the most of turning fifty, you'll want to focus on the people, places, activities, and things that actually mean the most to you.

That's what makes this book special. It's a flexible guide that will elicit different responses in everyone who uses it. It's designed so you can make the most of your milestone, given **your unique preferences and circumstances**.

Let's begin by putting things in perspective.

What's so Special about Fifty?

Twenty is a time of exploring. Thirty is a time of proving. Forty is a time of establishing.

Fifty is a time of reflecting, re-connecting, and re-grouping. It's a pivot point to the rest of our lives. It's the perfect opportunity to:

- appreciate your life thus far

- understand yourself better — examine your unique attributes and what's truly important to you

- do more of what you love — and less of what you don't

- strengthen important relationships

- treat yourself well

- have fun

- put things in order

- get rid of what you don't need

- live a life you love

- put things in place for the future, and

- establish your legacy

Of course, you don't need to do ALL of these things to have a terrific fiftieth year. This book is designed so you can focus on whatever is important to **you**.

Ж

How to Get the Most Out of This Book

1. This workbook is intended to be written on. Mark it up! Customize it. Make notes. Capture the ideas and plans you'd like to undertake during your fiftieth. Underline and highlight. Sketch and doodle. Use different colored pens and highlighters. Add Post-It notes, stickers, or other embellishments. Glue in images, words and phrases from magazines if you wish. Create your own personalized guide to your milestone year. Make this book yours. As new ideas occur to you, capture them in this handy, easily retrievable location.

2. Use the Contents at the beginning of this book as an overview of the "50 Ways to Enjoy Turning Fifty."

3. **Feel free to browse and bounce around the "50 Ways" however you like.** Focus on the sections that are most interesting to you. Skip over the ideas that are less relevant or appealing. Perhaps you'd like to focus on a chapter at a time — or one of the "50 Ways" per week. Maybe you'd like to open the book up to a random page at random times. It's completely up to you.

    This book features **"Key Questions"** for you to contemplate and answer as a way of gaining new insights about yourself and figuring out how to make the most of turning fifty.

    There are also **"Thought Experiments"** designed to plumb a little deeper. Ideally, you will set aside uninterrupted time to give these questions your full, focused attention.

    As well, there are **"Activities"** i.e. things for you to do.

4. The best way to get the most out of this book is by participating: If you actually write out your answers to the Key Questions and Thought Experiments, you will elicit more and better insights and ideas.

5. There are also extra pages at the back of this book where you can capture additional **Notes and Ideas** for enjoying your fiftieth year.

ACTIVITY:

Take a few minutes to scan the Contents at the beginning of this book.

Select which of the "50 Ways to Enjoy Turning Fifty" are most appealing to you.

Begin to customize your "50 Workbook" by putting checkmarks or stars or color-coded symbols beside the ideas that are most interesting to you.

BONUS:

If you'd like to receive free weekly self-quiz questions and self-coaching prompts via email, please sign up here: http://bit.ly/weeklyprompts

First Things First...

Before you can make the most of this milestone, you need to accept the fact that you are turning fifty years old. It's impossible to make a big, happy deal out of something you're dreading. So here's an important question: **Honestly — how do you feel about getting older?**

If you're looking forward to it, wonderful! Please proceed to the **next chapter** immediately.

If, in contrast, you're not utterly thrilled to be getting older, please read on.

Milestone years are a particularly nasty reminder of — there's no other way to say it — aging.

However, aging is the natural consequence of being alive. It happens to every cell in our bodies — and to every other body on the planet. Every living thing gets older. It's a biological fact.

In traditional cultures, people gain more respect as they age. They are venerated for their wisdom and life experience.

In our society, alas, there's a stigma around getting older. It's particularly acute here in Los Angeles. Here, aging is punishable by ostracism. Plastic surgery is an amateur sport. Real housewives make the television *Real Housewives* look like fossils.

Unfortunately, as the self-proclaimed Entertainment Capital of the World, what happens in L.A. infiltrates the planet via films, television, videos, magazines, and social media. People around the planet are bombarded with images of youthful faces and buff bodies as if those were normal.

It's not normal. Nor is it reality. Look around at the people you actually know. How many of them look as if they walked off a movie screen? Watch people at the grocery store — and compare them to the magazine images at the check-out stand.

What you see in the media is the result of (a) selective marketing of surprisingly tiny, extraordinarily beautiful people, plus (b) the handiwork of scores of publicity experts, personal trainers, stylists, makeup artists, hair stylists, lighting experts, camera operators, air brushers, and Photoshop experts all devoted to making their subjects look good. They are all in the business of creating illusion, not truth.

Let's shift our attention, then, to the truth.

The Truth Is...

- you are turning fifty years old

- time operates in only one direction i.e. you will not get younger

- if you don't accept the process of getting older, you're going to be miserable for the rest of your years

Make peace with getting older. Accept this thing you cannot change.

Ж

Here's the first of *50 Ways to Enjoy Turning Fifty:*

Way #1: Accept your age

Every age has its advantages and disadvantages. Let's begin by considering the upside of turning fifty.

"Now that I'm fifty, I don't put up with other people's crap anymore," observed Chris. "I've stopped worrying about what other people think."

When she turned fifty, Diane was tickled to be able to join AARP, making her eligible for lower insurance rates and countless shopping and travel discounts. Tom noticed a bevy of benefits: "I am enjoying walking instead of running, listening instead of pontificating, coaching basketball, sharing half a century's worth of eclectic discoveries with any and all and watching my daughter grow into a smart, talented, effervescent young woman. There are many life challenges of course, like aging parents, busy work and home lives, etc. but I meet them with confidence."

THOUGHT EXPERIMENT:	
Make a list of people you admire who are over fifty and who are living terrific lives. *This might include friends, family members, scientists, artists, celebrities, politicians, business people, colleagues, or others.*	Beside each name, jot down what you admire about how this person is living their life:

Key Questions:

1. What are some benefits of turning fifty? Make a list. *Include practical things (e.g., discounts) as well as the more esoteric (e.g., different life perspective).*

2. What are you looking forward to this year?

Now let's acknowledge the downside of getting older. We look older. Our bodies change. We move more slowly. We have less energy. We can be more forgetful or find it takes longer for us to recall information. We lose more loved ones.

Thought Experiment:

1. What concerns do you have about turning fifty?

2. What challenges are you experiencing or expecting?

3. Review your answers to questions 1 and 2. Of those, circle those things you can't change.

4. Pick one item you just circled. What constructive actions you can take regarding this item? *E.g., if you said "thinning hair" is something you don't like and can't change about turning fifty, you might answer this question with things such as "find headwear I like" or "go to the doctor to check out my options" or "learn to love my appearance at this or any age."*

Put a checkmark beside any constructive action you'd like to try. Make a point of doing it this month.

5. Pick another item you circled. What constructive actions can you take?

Put a checkmark beside any constructive action you'd like to try. Make a point of doing it this month.

ACTIVITY:

This week, make a point of observing your thoughts. Make a point of noticing when you make judgments about getting older.

When you do, pat yourself on the back! You caught yourself! Now shift your attention to the benefits of being fifty. (The items you wrote at the top of page 8.)

Next, consider how you might think differently about what's going on. Sure, there are things we might not enjoy about this age…but that is true for ANY age. Any phase of life has its plusses and minuses.

Take a moment to consider the alternative: You are alive. It wasn't too long ago in the history of humanity that people didn't live much past forty. In 1900, the world average life expectancy was thirty-one years of age. In 1950, it was forty-eight.

THOUGHT EXPERIMENT:

List people you know who did not live to see fifty. *Include people you knew personally as well as celebrities and public figures who left us too soon.*

Since you're still here on the planet, why not make the best of it?

You owe it to yourself to make the best of turning fifty. You can't change it. You might as well accept it.

Once you accept the fact you're turning fifty, why not make the best of the situation? Why not use this milestone as an opportunity to have a great year?

I mean, you *could* continue on as you are and make fifty indistinguishable from forty-nine. Or, if you prefer, you could make this year *better*.

With relatively minor adjustments, it's possible to make your fiftieth year more enjoyable than last year. With a few decisions and commitments, you can make this a great twelve months. In fact, if you decide to, you can make this your *best year ever*.

Ж

Here's the second of *50 Ways to Enjoy Turning Fifty:*

Way #2: Decide to make your fiftieth year special

This is perhaps the simplest yet most important activity in this book: to choose to make your fiftieth a great year. If you start out with that intention, you are well on your way to making the most of your experiences over the next twelve months.

It's completely up to you.

ACTIVITY:

Decide to make this year special. Promise yourself a wonderful year. *(Bonus points if you write out a detailed commitment to yourself.)*

ACTIVITY:

Tell people about your impending Fiftieth Birthday. Let them know you intend to make it a special year.

THOUGHT EXPERIMENT:

1. As fast as possible, write out reasons why you deserve to have a special year.

   ➤

   ➤

   ➤

   ➤

   ➤

2. What kinds of things would constitute a special year for you? Which activities or events? Where? With whom?

3. Clear five minutes for some imagining: Pretend that it's the day before your fifty-first birthday. You are pleased and proud of the year you've just had. Really, it's the best year you've ever had. Answer the following questions, being as detailed as possible:

    *   What's happened over the past twelve months?

    *   What have you experienced?

    *   What places, people, and activities have been a part of your fiftieth year?

In the next chapter, we'll take these initial ideas and expand on them so you can plan your best year ever.

Chapter 2

Planning Your Best Year Ever

Think about your fiftieth year, overall. What kind of year would you like it to be?

Ж

Here's another of *50 Ways to Enjoy Turning Fifty:*

Way #3: Pick a theme for your year

What is your number one priority? What kind of tone would you like to set? If you gave your year a theme, what would it be?

My number one priority was to have fun. Keith's was to focus on his health. Maria's was to relax. Maybe yours is to travel. Or to learn. Or to create. Or to do good deeds. Perhaps you'd like this to be the "Year of Music." Maybe you've been overly career driven and this is the year you've like to give more attention to "Home."

ACTIVITY:

What kind of year would you like your fiftieth to be? Choose a word or phrase to capture the overarching theme — or top priority — for the next twelve months. *(E.g., "Fun", "Relaxation", "Learning", "Philanthropy", "Music", "Home", "Adventure")*

Write your theme below and doodle around it. Sketch images. Jot down words and phrases that pop into your head when you think about your theme.

If you'd like, flip through some magazines and clip out words or images that reflect your theme. Make a collage and/or glue them here.

Here's the next of *50 Ways to Enjoy Turning Fifty:*

Way #4: Plan a great birthday

How do you want to spend your actual birthday? Do you want a big shindig? A romantic dinner? A special trip? Do you want to try skydiving or go-karting on your birthday? Would you like to go fishing or play eighteen holes or see a Broadway show? Do you have a hankering to play poker or make a sculpture or play volleyball or go to the spa?

What would be the most enjoyable for you? How do you want to mark the occasion?

Kari spent her birthday in Ireland — home of her ancestry. Andre took over a restaurant for a huge party. John climbed Half Dome at Yosemite National Park. Abby opted for a quiet dinner in a favorite restaurant. Bill invited fifty of his closest friends to a culinary school for an evening of cooking haute cuisine.

In an ideal world, I would have loved to have gathered together the people I care about most on my fiftieth for a huge shindig with great music, tasty treats, and ample libations. Alas, practicalities prevented me from doing any of that. Instead, I spent my birthday with my family experiencing my first two frolics of the year — a hike in the high desert plus a romp on the beach.

It wasn't the "dream birthday" of my fantasies but it was a very fun day. Actually, it was the best birthday I'd had in many years. Even better: My "Fifty Frolics" project was off to a terrific start. I was heartened to know that the celebration was just beginning – and that I had the next twelve months — and (at least) forty-eight more frolics — to make the most of turning fifty.

KEY QUESTION:

List appealing ways you could celebrate your actual birthday.

➢

➢

➢

➢

Review your list. Circle your favorite of these options.

ACTIVITIES:

1. Make special plans for your Fiftieth Birthday. Incorporate what you can from your list, making relevant practical adjustments.

2. On the day you turn fifty, enjoy and savor the day.

3. Capture an image of yourself on the day (e.g., a photo, a painting, a video, a blog post, or something else to remember your Fiftieth Birthday.)

Ж

Here's the next of *50 Ways to Enjoy Turning Fifty:*

Way #5: Identify activities you'd like to be a part of your fiftieth year

---

Think beyond your actual birthday into the next twelve months: What activities would you like to experience throughout the year?

Joanie ran a marathon. Karl got a tattoo. Angelica wanted to take classes in something she hadn't done before — like Bikram Yoga. Ming researched the possible concerts and theatrical productions he wanted to see during his fiftieth. Book-lover Sue compiled a reading list for her year.

KEY QUESTIONS:

1. What activities would you like to do during your fiftieth year?

---

2. Think about your theme for the year (page 13). Brainstorm theme-related activities you'd like to do this year.

If there's something you aren't able to make a part of your actual birthday, can you find a way to make it part of your fiftieth year? For example, I wasn't able to gather together my best friends for my birthday since they were scattered geographically…but I was able to visit with many of them throughout the year.

KEY QUESTIONS:

1. Imagine your "Ideal Birthday." In a perfect world, if there were no practical constraints, how would you spend your fiftieth? Write down all the details.

2. What elements of your "Ideal Birthday" can you incorporate during your fiftieth year?

When Carolyn thought about what was most important and interesting to her, she thought of politics. She used her fiftieth as an excuse to get more involved volunteering in local elections. By the time she was fifty-one, she was running for office herself.

THOUGHT EXPERIMENT:

Think about the following areas of life. For each, jot down relevant activities you'd like to do this year. In each category, what do you want to do, honor, learn, or explore this year?

- career / professional / financial

- family / domestic

- social

- learning / education / personal development

- health / fitness

- leisure activities / hobbies / long-term interests

- life dreams

Here's the next of *50 Ways to Enjoy Turning Fifty:*

Way #6: Identify who you'd like to be a part of your year

You owe it to yourself to spend time during your fiftieth year with people you love and who love you.

Now this *might* include family members but it might not. Rather than being with whomever society says you "should" love and who "should" love you, aim to be with people who make your heart sing just to think of them. Folks who make you laugh and smile. Those who make you feel like you're being your best possible self.

KEY QUESTIONS:

1. Who is most important in your life? Who do you really truly love?

2. Who brings you joy? Who makes your heart sing?

3. With whom do you love talking?

4. With whom do you love spending time?

5. Who supports you? Who gives you comfort?

6. To whom do you turn for guidance?

7. When you think back over the previous five decades, who has been most important in your life?

8. Think ahead: As you imagine your fifties, sixties, seventies and beyond, who do you expect will be most important to you?

ACTIVITIES:

1. Review your answers on page 19. Circle the names of the people with whom you'd like to spend time during your fiftieth year.

2. Contact them and start making plans to get together. Is there an opportunity for a fun weekend gathering of buddies? Perhaps it's time for a romantic getaway. Or a family adventure. Or a heart-to-heart with a lifelong chum. Is there a reunion you could attend or plan?

3. Who on your list are you unlikely to be able to see in person? How can you connect with them long distance? Make plans to call, Facetime, Skype, email, write, or otherwise communicate with them during the year.

Ж

Here's the next of *50 Ways to Enjoy Turning Fifty:*

Way #7: Reach out to hidden gems in your past

Sometimes we don't like thinking about past life chapters for fear of traipsing into negative memories. However, if you take the plunge, you will find "hidden gems" in every chapter of your life. For every "jerk" not worth remembering, there are also some kind people — friends at the time — with whom you've lost contact for no particular reason.

If you choose to, you can use your fiftieth year to reconnect with these lost, hidden gems in your past.

Facebook and other social media are great for this, but personally, I prefer using the phone. It's more personal and interactive.

It's possible — and fun — to pick up the phone and call anyone from your past.

Of course, it's helpful if you give some context when you reach them: "This is a voice from your past. It's [insert the name they knew you by] from [insert the place where you knew each other]." You don't need an excuse other than "I was thinking about you and thought I'd call. Is now a good time to chat?"

Using this completely obvious and easy technique, I've reconnected with some wonderful people with whom I'd had no contact in decades. These phone calls lead to other rewarding conversations and fun visits. I highly recommend it.

It's pretty sweet to receive these calls, too. During my fiftieth year, Harry — my long-lost housemate from grad school — tracked me down and called me, out of the blue. It was so good to hear Harry's voice! It meant so much to reconnect and to learn about his wonderful life in Texas. It warmed my heart to know that he cared enough to track me down.

ACTIVITY:

Is there anyone you'd like to reach out to during this year? Who do you remember fondly from the past? Is there anyone with whom you're not presently in contact but would like to be?

Pick one person.

Find their number. *(If you can't find their information by searching online, ask someone who might know how to reach them — perhaps a mutual friend or relative.)*

Call them.

Ж

Here's the next of *50 Ways to Enjoy Turning Fifty:*

Way #8: **Make plans to be in meaningful places this year**

Take a moment to think about the places that are most important to you. It might be your hometown or where you went to school or places you visited with someone you love. Perhaps there's a location where you felt particularly happy. Maybe there's a destination you have always wanted to visit but haven't yet.

Why not use turning fifty as an excuse to visit the places you love — and the places you'd love to go?

Ellen's fondest memories are of childhood summers spent in Rhode Island, so she rented a beach house there for a month during her fiftieth. Dan felt called to visit his family in Colorado. Katherine had yearned to see Antarctica during her life, so she found a way to get there during her fiftieth year by performing music on a cruise ship.

Me? I'm a "water baby." Being near water makes me happy. The sound soothes me. My childhood summers were spent swimming, canoeing, waterskiing, and otherwise frolicking in and around water. My preferred travel getaway is anywhere with a waterfront.

When I turned fifty, I realized that although I was living on the West Coast, I wasn't taking advantage of my location. The beach was forty whole blocks away — a twenty minute drive each way — so I tended not to go there. How ridiculous!

I used my birthday as an excuse to change that: I went kayaking and canoeing. I made a regular practice of taking my dogs to the beach — (twenty minute drive, be damned) — so we could walk along the shoreline. Basically, I used turning fifty as an opportunity to spend more time in places I loved.

So can you.

KEY QUESTIONS:

1. What places do you love? What locations are special to you? Where have you been happiest?

2. Which settings soothe you?

3. Are there destinations you have not yet visited yet feel drawn to? Where would you love to go someday?

ACTIVITIES:

1. Review your answers on page 22. Circle the places that you want to make a part of your fiftieth year.

2. Find ways to incorporate these locations into your fiftieth year.

Ж

Here's the next of *50 Ways to Enjoy Turning Fifty:*

Way #9: Schedule "Special Days" throughout the year

Guess what? You're allowed to have more than one special day a year.

In addition to your fiftieth birthday, consider any of the following:

Personal Days - *to do whatever you wish or whatever you need*

A true personal day is a gift you give yourself. When you take a Personal Day, the idea is to ask yourself, "What do I really, truly need *today*?" Maybe you need to nap. Or perhaps there is a little voice in your head telling you to spend the day in your PJs, watching schlock TV. Are you yearning to spend time in nature? Are you feeling so behind on something that it would be a relief to spend a day getting caught up?

Play Days - *devoted to having fun*

What's fun for you? It might be a day trip. Eighteen holes. A jaunt to the beach. Hours exploring art galleries.

Theme Days - *devoted to activities connected to whatever you selected for your theme for this year*

For example, if your theme for your fiftieth year is "Relax", then your Theme Days would be devoted to doing just that. If your theme is "Learning" then you'd schedule classes or workshops or reading days.

Celebration Days - *to honor important events*

These might be traditional — things like anniversaries or birthdays or calendar holidays. Or they might be celebrations of your own devising. What would *you* like to honor? What qualities or accomplishments or anniversaries or traditions would you like to make a part of your fiftieth year?

For example, I like to celebrate the anniversary of the day I defended my doctoral dissertation. It felt like a big accomplishment to earn my Ph.D. before the age of thirty. It was made more meaningful because family and friends drove for five to eight hours to be there. Their smiling faces were sprinkled throughout the audience when I presented my data to the department. We had a terrific party that night, too — great eats and fun festivities. In the years since, I've made it a point to recognize and celebrate this personal anniversary.

KEY QUESTIONS:

1. List possible options for future Play Days. What would be fun for you?

2. List options for possible Theme Days during your fiftieth year.

3. List options for possible Celebration Days you'd like to have this year.

4. What other special events, birthdays, or anniversaries do you want to make a point of celebrating during your fiftieth year?

ACTIVITIES:

1. Right now, pull out your calendar or planner and put a big star on (at least) four random days during the year. When those days roll around, make a point of enjoying a Personal Day, a Play Day, a Theme Day, or a Celebration Day.

2. While your planner is out, highlight important events, birthdays, or anniversaries you want to make note of during your fiftieth year. This year, make a point of making them true celebrations.

Ж

Here's the next of *50 Ways to Enjoy Turning Fifty:*

Way #10: Identify what creative input you'd like this year

Are you a bookworm? A film fanatic? A music aficionado? A dance devotee? A gallery geek?

Part of making the most of your fiftieth year is ensuring that you are enjoying the arts that mean most to you.

For example, if you love reading, you could make a list of books you've wanted to read but haven't yet — or ask your friends for book recommendations. You could go through your bookshelves to make a reading pile out of your favorite books. You could join a book club or start a reading group. You could find a "book buddy" with whom to discuss books you both read. You could aim to read a particular number of books during your milestone year.

If you are a concert-goer, you could see where and when your favorite performers are touring. Marlene drove to a city eight hours away so she could see Steve Martin playing his Grammy-award winning bluegrass music live.

"The patter was perfect," she reported. "The music was superb. I'm so glad I went!"

If you can't see your favorite performers in person, see if they have any new CDs or MP3s available. Or just spend some focused time listening to the music you've already got. Mine your music collection for your favorites.

If you're preferred entertainment is TV, make a point of indulging in your favorite shows. Or check out acclaimed series you may have missed that are now available on DVDs or online.

KEY QUESTIONS:

1. What are the arts you enjoy?

2. How can you incorporate the arts you enjoy into your fiftieth year?

ACTIVITY:

Go online to see if your favorite musical artists are performing anywhere near you during your fiftieth year. Do they have any new CDs or MP3s available?

ACTIVITY:

Make yourself a "mix tape" in honor of turning fifty. Compile your favorite songs into an MP3 playlist or onto a CD-Rom (or cassette if you want to be all vintage about it). Include songs that tell your story — the songs that have had significance for you and your life.

ACTIVITY:

Go through your books. Put aside those you'd like to read this year. Keep an eye out for old faves you'd like to re-read and also for books you own but haven't yet read.

ACTIVITY:

Ask your friends to recommend books, music, films, and/or television shows they've enjoyed recently. Keep a list of ones that appeal in the **Notes and Ideas Pages** at the end of this book.

ACTIVITY:

Browse in shops or online for new finds. Seek out award nominees, prize winners, "Top Ten" lists, and "Year's Best" lists for inspiration. Keep track of the music, books, films, and television shows that interest you in the **Notes and Ideas Pages** at the end of this book.

Chapter 3

Implementing Your Plan for Your Best Year Ever

You've generated ideas for enjoying your fiftieth year. You've identified what you want to do with your year, where you wish to be, and with whom. Now it's a matter of implementing your plans. That's the focus of this chapter.

Ж

Here's the next of *50 Ways to Enjoy Turning Fifty:*

> ## *Way #11:* Start. Do the things you love.

Begin. It's that simple. You've identified what you want to do with your year, where you wish to be, and with whom. Start. Make it so.

ACTIVITY:

Review your ideas and plans for turning fifty. Re-read what you've written so far in this workbook. Highlight whatever appeals most.

As your Milestone year commences, start doing the things you've chosen. Call people you care about to get together. Just do it. Enjoy yourself!

(Should you have difficulty getting started, review your responses on page 11. You deserve to enjoy a wonderful year.)

Here's the next of *50 Ways to Enjoy Turning Fifty:*

Way #12: Keep track of how you're doing

To actually accomplish your plans, it's helpful to keep track of how you're doing. Jot down details on your calendar or in this book. Mark big checkmarks — or stick gold stars — beside all the ideas you've had that you actually do.

What's worked for you in the past to keep yourself on track?

Rafe wanted to golf more during his fiftieth year, so he put different colored stickers on his calendar to represent each time he got in nine or eighteen holes.

Debra wanted to lose fifty pounds during her fiftieth year. She lost ninety (!) by checking in each day with a diet buddy and by attending weight loss meetings at least once per week.

When I turned fifty, I had so many things I wanted to do during the year, I kept track of everything using an Excel spreadsheet. Each column documented a different goal or project. As the year unfolded, I made note of the books I read, the music I listened to, the frolics I experienced, and so on. I highlighted any projects that were falling behind in yellow. This way I could see, at a glance, what was getting done and what wasn't — and I could take action, accordingly.

KEY QUESTIONS:

1. What's worked well for you in the past to keep yourself on track?

2. How could you use these tools or techniques to keep yourself on track with your plans for your fiftieth?

Here's the next of *50 Ways to Enjoy Turning Fifty:*

Way #13: **Prepare for possible obstacles and interference**

If you're like most people, you'll begin your fiftieth year with some celebrations and some fun activities.

The important thing is to KEEP GOING. This is where some people get stuck.

To keep yourself on track, it's helpful to identify what potential obstacles might arise that could sideline your plans — so you can prepare yourself accordingly. A little forethought can act like "obstacle inoculation."

Consider these Possible Obstacles:

1. Slipping back into old habits.

It's funny how you can be full of mad resolve, embarking on a new initiative…and then, a few weeks later, notice that you're back to doing the same ol' same ol'.

For example, one of my initiatives for my fiftieth year was to indulge in (at least) fifty treats. I started out great on my birthday, purchasing fresh cut flowers and special ingredients for my birthday dinner…and yet within the first month, I faltered. However, because I was keeping track of my commitments using Ye Olde Excel Spreadsheet, I noticed that I had only enjoyed two treats in the first four weeks. I promptly booked a massage…and I relied on my spreadsheet to help keep me on track for the rest of the year.

KEY QUESTIONS:

1. How will you keep yourself on track with your Milestone plans?

2. How can you set up reminders or periodic reviews to stay on track?

---

2. Taking on too much.

Are you someone who tends to take on too much, then gets overwhelmed? This section is for you. (Otherwise, please skip ahead to the next page.)

As someone who is "interested in many things", I tend to overextend myself. My fiftieth birthday plans were no exception. I wanted to enjoy (at least) Fifty Frolics during the year plus read (at least) fifty books plus try (at least) fifty new recipes plus see (at least) fifty films plus…you get the idea.

The key was to prioritize. More than anything I wanted to have fun during the year, so my Fifty Frolics project was my number one priority. Anything else was gravy. My other projects were extra treats rather than onerous obligations. If they happened, they happened and I enjoyed them. If I fell short in the actual number, it really didn't matter. The point was to have fun during the year.

I felt comfortable with the commitment to enjoy Fifty Frolics because it was basically a goal of one adventure per week. I knew that I could meet my goal even when work and domestic responsibilities and other random things swelled to fill my schedule. If I had to miss a frolic during a given week, it was easy enough to make it up during the subsequent week or two.

Take a moment to review your ideas and plans for your fiftieth. What is your theme? What is your number one priority? What is secondary? To what extent are your plans practical and doable, given your current situation? To what extent are your plans pleasing and easy? To what extent are your plans overwhelming or overambitious? What adjustments are needed?

ACTIVITY:

1. Review your theme or top priority. What do you most want to happen this year?

2. Identify what is secondary. What would be "nice" or "a bonus" but is less important to you?

3. To what extent are your plans reasonable, given your personal circumstances and schedule? What adjustments are needed? Modify your plans so you have a clear and pleasant game plan for your fiftieth.

---

3. Negative people — or "Wet Blankets" — or "Doubters" — or "Haters"

As excited as you may be about your Fiftieth Projects, other people might have different reactions. Some may find your plans less interesting than you do. They may change the subject. Others may think you're being foolish or self-indulgent. Other people might not really have much of a reaction at all.

Without meaning to, these responses may dampen your enthusiasm. They might cause you to doubt or scuttle your plans. Don't let them. These are YOUR plans to make YOUR Milestone the year you want it to be.

KEY QUESTIONS:

1. What will you do if you encounter negative responses to your plans for your Milestone?

2. What will do if you experience lukewarm or indifferent reactions to your plans?

---

4. Life Intervenes

Whenever people embark on new initiatives, life tends to push back. Work demands or family matters or random other things often conspire to interfere with our endeavors. Whenever this happens, you can either allow yourself to get derailed or you can use it as an opportunity to review and re-commit to your plans.

Case in point: My mother passed away unexpectedly during my fiftieth year. Poof! Everything in my personal and professional life had to be put on hold while I dealt with all that needed attention.

It's an extreme example, but smaller things — an illness, a move, an unprecedented event — can also affect commitment and progress on any project. So what can you do to stay on track with your plans for your fiftieth year, no matter what?

In my case, I went public. I wrote about my "Fiftieth" commitments in a blog for the whole world to see and hold me accountable.

Besides, sometimes these unexpected curveballs have silver linings. For example, the passing of my mother was a profoundly sad event yet, weirdly, it provided opportunities that made my milestone a very special year. Going through my mother's house provided a vivid way to look back on my first five decades. I was given opportunities to look within and to look at life differently. My priorities shifted. I changed how I wanted to be living my life. I made a point of connecting with important people in my life, of expressing gratitude, of giving, of putting things in order, and of getting rid of things I didn't need. My life changed in countless, meaningful ways during my milestone year. My experiences enriched the ideas in this book. My hope is that you are finding it helpful. If so, that would be the best silver lining to emerge from this very dark cloud in my life.

THOUGHT EXPERIMENT:

Think of a time life intervened with your plans.

1. How did you respond?

2. To what extent were you derailed?

3. What helped you get back on track?

4. What would you do differently, were you to be in that situation again?

---

5. Other Obstacles

What other interference or obstacles are likely to arise as you embark on your Milestone year? What tends to crop up in your life?

Most importantly: How do you tend to get in your own way? How do you tend to self-sabotage your plans? How will you manage these tendencies?

THOUGHT EXPERIMENT:

List possible obstacles that might affect your plans to have a great fiftieth year. *Include ways in which you may self-sabotage yourself.*	Brainstorm solutions for each. *Consider what's worked well for you in the past as well as new solutions you'd like to try.*

Here's the next of *50 Ways to Enjoy Turning Fifty:*

Way #14: Adjust your plans as you go

A key part of making plans, keeping yourself on track, and managing the obstacles that arise is to make adjustments as things unfold.

Maybe something is going so well, you want to do more of it. By all means, change your plans to do more.

Perhaps you're not enjoying something you thought you would. Then, obviously, you'd stop.

Maybe you misjudged the time necessary for your plans. If you aimed to read a novel a week, for example, but "only" read five during the year, who cares? You read five books!

If you've been over-ambitious in your plans, it's fine to scale back. Avoid stress and frustration. **The point of your "Fiftieth Projects" and plans is to make your fiftieth year pleasant and enjoyable.** Make whatever adjustments are needed along the way.

For example, I had planned to take fifty art classes during the year. It seemed a no-brainer, given that I've taken art classes every semester for the past several decades. However my fiftieth year was not a typical year. I had to fly back and forth the 3000 miles to take care of things after my mother passed away. A few months into my fiftieth year, it was clear I wouldn't get to one art class, let alone fifty. I mean, I *could* have taken a class…but not without it being overly stressful. So I let myself off the hook: I didn't make it to a single art class that year — and that was okay.

Again, the point is to have a great, pleasant fiftieth year. As it unfolds, make whatever adjustments make sense to you.

ACTIVITY:

Pull out your calendar or planner. Schedule a time, two months after your fiftieth birthday to review your plans on page 37.

Ж

ACTIVITY:

Two months after your fiftieth birthday, return here to review how your plans are unfolding:

- What's working well?

- What's not?

- What do you want to do less of?

- What do you want to do more of?

- What adjustments do you need to make to ensure a great milestone year?

Here's the next of *50 Ways to Enjoy Turning Fifty:*

Way #15: Chronicle your year

Hey, you only turn fifty once — and you're making all these cool plans for your milestone — so why not make note of how you spend it?

Document your fiftieth year in a way that's pleasing to you. You could keep a journal to chronicle your activities, thoughts, and insights. You'll probably take photos. You might make sketches. You could collect ticket stubs and whatnot to compile a scrapbook. You could create a collage or a wall display.

Once again, the key point here is that this should be fun and enjoyable — not an onerous obligation. Lois made a point of taking tons of photos throughout the year. I wrote a blog. Ellen made an online scrapbook to document her special birthday month in Rhode Island. Don, a clever lyricist, captured key events in song.

ACTIVITY:

Decide on a fun way to document your fiftieth year — and do it.

ACTIVITY:

Create or commission a portrait of yourself at fifty. It might be a photo, a painting, a cartoon, or some other rendering. For example, you can get a cartoon of yourself drawn for $6 at www.fiverr.com.

ACTIVITY: CREATE A MILESTONE MEMORY BANK

1. Designate a container to be your Milestone Memory Bank. This might be a large empty jar or a box with a removable lid or anything else that can hold 52 folded pieces of paper. (Decorate it if you wish.)

2. Start a new habit: Each Sunday, write on a piece of paper (at least) one good thing you've experienced that week. Fold the paper and put it your Memory Bank.

3. On your fifty-first birthday, read the contents of your Memory Bank.

Chapter 4

Treating Yourself Well

How do you treat yourself? Are you your own best friend/cheerleader/number one fan? Do you regularly enjoy simple pleasures — or indulge in downright treats? Are you taking good care of yourself — mind, body, and spirit? Do you give yourself personal time? Do you have fairly good balance in your life? If so, well done! Please move on to Chapter Five.

If, however, you would benefit from treating yourself better, then why not use your fiftieth year as an opportunity to do so?

Ж

Here's the next of *50 Ways to Enjoy Turning Fifty:*

Way #16: Indulge in simple pleasures

What are your favorite simple pleasures? What are the little things that give you joy in your life?

What music do you enjoy? Are there particular foods that make you happy? In either case there might be something from your childhood — or something you've discovered more recently — that you adore. Little treats to enrich your day.

Julia buys herself a fresh bouquet every week. Matt treats himself to music. Maria splurges on art magazines that catch her eye.

Many simple pleasures don't cost a cent. Keisha's favorite simple pleasure is to take a nap. For Paulo, it's a treat whenever he's outside…even better if he can walk on a beach or spend time reading outdoors.

I have fond memories from decades ago of receiving a card from a former landlady. Enclosed was $5. "Go buy yourself some flowers," she wrote, so I did. I can't adequately express how much joy that five bucks gave me. I went to the market and carefully selected flowers I knew my landlady would have chosen. I took them home and placed them prominently in my wee apartment. Every time they caught my eye, I smiled. A simple, true source of pleasure.

KEY QUESTIONS:

1. As fast as you can, list simple pleasures you love. What treats give you joy?

> ➤

> ➤

> ➤

> ➤

> ➤

> ➤

> ➤

> ➤

> ➤

> ➤

2. Now, think about your fiftieth year. How can you indulge in more simple pleasures, going forward?

ACTIVITIES:

1. Make a list of your favorite childhood foods.

2. Make a point of having one item from your list this week.

3. During your fiftieth year, make a point of eating more of your favorite childhood foods.

THOUGHT EXPERIMENT:

1. Think about treats others have given you. What kindnesses have given you joy?

2. How can you give yourself similar treats?

Here's the next of *50 Ways to Enjoy Turning Fifty:*

Way #17: Nurture yourself

Do you take good care of yourself? If so, carry on and move ahead to the next section.

If, however, you're giving yourself short shrift, you can use this milestone year to change that.

Marti treats herself to weekly massages. Phillip would rather eat glass than have strangers touch him so spa treatments are the opposite of "nurturing" for him. Instead his self-care involves taking quiet, private, thinking time. Every day he clears a half hour to step away from stresses and responsibilities and just "be."

KEY QUESTIONS:

1. To what extent are you taking good care of yourself?

2. What's working well in your self-care?

3. What gaps need to be addressed?

---

4. List self-care or self-nurturing activities you could do this year.

➢

➢

➢

➢

➢

➢

➢

➢

➢

➢

5. Review your list and circle the items that are most appealing.

6. Make a point of doing them during your milestone year.

Ж

Here's the next of *50 Ways to Enjoy Turning Fifty:*

Way #18: Attend to your health

How's your health? Do you go for regular medical and dental check-ups? Have you had your vision checked recently? When health issues arise, do you attend to them promptly?

We need to give some attention to our bodies — it's basic maintenance. Just like you give your car regular oil changes, it's important to give your body regular attention.

If you aren't very health conscious, now is good time to start. The better you take care of your body, the longer you'll be living happily and healthily.

KEY QUESTIONS:

1. Describe your current overall health.

2. What physical changes have you noticed over the past few years?

3. How have you responded?

On page 45 is a chart for you to contemplate different areas of your current physical health.

Aspects of Health	Describe the current state of this aspect of your health.	What are your healthy habits or practices in this area?	What are you doing that is unhelpful or unhealthy?
Energy			
Physical Strength			
Physical Flexibility			
Balance			
Endurance			
Metabolism			
Sleep			
Dental			
Skin			
Food consumption			
Beverage consumption			
Use of prescribed medications			
Self-medication			

KEY QUESTION:

Review your answers on page 44 and 45. What needs to be addressed?

When he turned fifty, John wanted to improve his eating habits. He committed to make a point of eating at least one salad a day. Cathy started keeping track to ensure she was drinking enough water daily. Margaret made a commitment to make annual appointments with a dermatologist for a total body "skin check" to ensure nothing was out of the ordinary. Keith completely transformed his body thanks to barefoot running and the Paleo diet.

THOUGHT EXPERIMENT:

1. List five healthful actions you could take this year.

    ➢

    ➢

    ➢

    ➢

    ➢

2. List five healthy habits you could start.

    ➢

    ➢

    ➢

    ➢

    ➢

3. Circle the items that are most appealing. Make a point of doing them during your fiftieth year.

Here's the next of *50 Ways to Enjoy Turning Fifty:*

Way #19: Identify the fitness activities you'd like to be a part of this year

---

You may have already incorporated your favorite sports or fitness activities in your plans for your fiftieth year. If you're like Al — physically fit and proud of his fifty-year- old body — please move on to the next section.

If you aren't, here's an opportunity to do so. You know what? You're turning fifty. If fitness isn't yet a part of your life, you're missing out on immediate health benefits and risking unnecessary problems as you get older.

Research has shown that to the extent you are physically active, the healthier you are, the happier you are, the higher your cognitive functioning, and the longer you live. In interviewing people for this book, I found a marked difference between those who were more sedentary and those who were more physically active. Members of the latter group were more vibrant, looked younger, and had a much more positive outlook. Many of them reported that they noticed the same difference among their friends and family members.

Being more physically active doesn't mean you have to embark on an Olympic training routine. It could be a matter of walking more. Or gardening. Or taking a stretching class. Or joining a friend to play badminton/squash/golf/croquet or something else that appeals. Or playing with your grandchildren. Or using a Wii Fit program, a FitBit, or a fitness app.

The idea is to find fun, easy ways to

- move your body more

- stretch / improve your flexibility

- strengthen your body

- practice or improve your balance

Or you could be more ambitious. Katherine set — and met — a goal of being able to do fifty pushups by her fifty-first birthday. Sam made a point of walking 10,000 steps a day, as measured by his pedometer. Kari developed new strength, tone, balance, and flexibility through regular yoga classes. Her energy level went through the roof. (And yowza did she look good!)

KEY QUESTIONS:

1. What fitness activities have you enjoyed in the past?

2. What fitness activities do you currently enjoy?

3. How could you be more physically active this year?

4. How could you improve your strength?

5. How could you improve your balance?

6. How could you improve your flexibility?

ACTIVITIES:

1. Review your list and circle the items that are most appealing.

2. During your fiftieth year, make a point of doing the items you circled.

Ж

Here's the next of *50 Ways to Enjoy Turning Fifty:*

Way #20: Stretch your mind

One alarming thing we tend to notice as we get older: Our brains seem to be working more slowly. Sometimes we can't find things we just had in our hands. Sometimes we have difficulty retrieving the correct word or name or phrase. (The technical name for this "anomia" and it is most annoying.)

Thankfully, recent research has shown that one reason older people take longer to remember something is because our brains have more in them. The retrieval processes are more challenged because there's so much more data to mine to find the information we're seeking.

Turning fifty is a great time to stretch our minds by doing things such as:

- learning something new *(online, in classes or workshops, or by other means)*

- reading

- doing puzzles of all sorts

- playing word or logic games

Louisa spent part of her fiftieth year learning Italian. Abby digs doing crossword puzzles. Chad enjoys taking philosophy courses online. Jean-Guy is a sucker for Sudoku. I adore playing word games on my iPad.

What about you?

ACTIVITY:

1. Write down fun ways you could stretch your mind this year.

2. Review your list and circle the items that are most appealing.

3. Make a point of doing them during your fiftieth year.

Here's the next of *50 Ways to Enjoy Turning Fifty:*

Way #21: **Nourish your spirit**

By "spirit", I mean that part of you, deep down. Spiritual practices feed your inner being.

Your fiftieth year can be an opportunity to nourish your spirit by doing things like:

- spending time in nature

- meditating

- expressing daily gratitude

- reading inspirational texts

- listening to inspirational songs or speakers

- participating in groups or organizations that your find spiritually fulfilling

Keira takes long walks in the forest to center herself. Every day, Mary Jane writes down ten things for which she's grateful. When he turned fifty, José started singing in the church choir.

KEY QUESTIONS:

1. What is soothing for you?

continued →

2. What makes your inner being calm and content?

3. What spirit-nourishing activities have you enjoyed in the past?

4. What else could you do this year to soothe your spirit?

5. Review your lists and circle the items that are most appealing.

6. Make a point of doing them during your milestone year.

Chapter 5

Having Fun

Regardless of the theme you've chosen for your fiftieth year, why not make a point of having fun this year? Play! Try new things. Flex your creativity. Use turning fifty as an opportunity to have fun.

Ж

Here's the next of *50 Ways to Enjoy Turning Fifty:*

Way #22: Play

Every child, every puppy, every young animal loves to play. Some of us continue to play throughout our lives. Others get wrapped up in school and work and achieving particular goals and taking care of our responsibilities and before we know it, poof! We're turning fifty — serious and sullen and stressed out.

Guess what? Turning fifty is a great time to reacquaint yourself with the delights — and rewards — of playtime.

Why play?

- it gives you energy

- it gives you new ideas

- it relieves stress

- it's a great way to bond with others — to make new friends or deepen the connections you already have

- you'll enjoy your life more

- you'll be more pleasant to be around

- it's fun

- it's good for your body, mind, and spirit

Doreen loved making paper maché crafts when she was a kid. To do so as an adult was a hoot. Peter was a board game junkie during college. When he turned fifty, he reacquainted himself with *Scrabble, Boggle,* and *Risk* and he sought out new board games to enjoy.

ACTIVITY:

1. What were your favorite games and play activities during childhood?

2. What were your favorite games and play activities during your teens?

   Your twenties?

   Your thirties?

   Your forties?

3. Review your lists and circle the items that are most appealing.

4. Make a point of doing them during your fiftieth year.

Here's the next of *50 Ways to Enjoy Turning Fifty:*

Way #23: Try something new

At this point in life, we've figured out a lot about what we like and what we don't like. As we do, there's a natural tendency for us to get stuck in well-worn ruts.

Yet there's a whole lot of undiscovered territory available to us. It's very freeing — and fun — to make a point of trying new things.

During her fiftieth year, Marcia tried paddleboarding for the first time. Carl haunted the Farmers Market looking for unusual fruits and vegetables he hadn't tasted before. Karen signed up for an improv comedy class.

Are there any activities you haven't tried yet but would like to? Surfing, playing a musical instrument, making chocolates, wood-turning, tap dancing, horseback riding — anything? Make a point of trying at least one new activity this year.

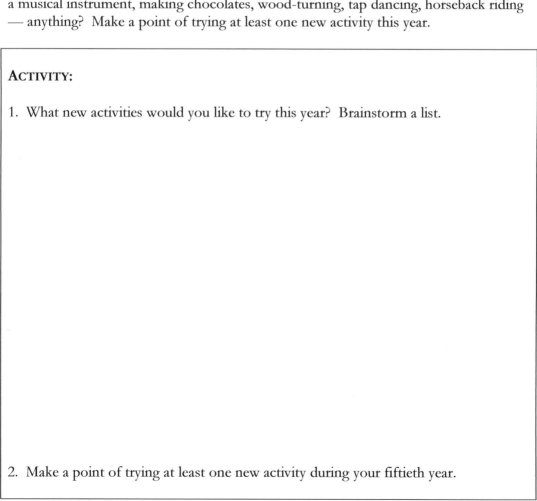

ACTIVITY:

1. What new activities would you like to try this year? Brainstorm a list.

2. Make a point of trying at least one new activity during your fiftieth year.

ACTIVITY:

Go to a book store or library. Browse the magazine racks for topics you know nothing about. Capture some new ideas.

ACTIVITY:

Go to the grocery store or a Farmer's Market. Find a fruit or vegetable you haven't eaten before. Take it home and try it. *(If you need help, search online for relevant recipes and preparation instructions.)*

ACTIVITY:

Put together a new outfit — something that's completely different from your typical attire — and wear it for a day. Just for fun. Spend the day as a cowboy or an artist or a nerd or a hippie or a Real Housewife or a business tycoon or whatever other "alter ego" you'd like to experience.

ACTIVITY:

Is there a new project you could start? Maybe there's something you've wanted to do for a long time but haven't. Go ahead. This is your opportunity.

ACTIVITY:

Go to www.youtube.com. Type any question you have into the search box. Browse among the resulting videos. Learn something new.

ACTIVITY:

Go to a restaurant. (Bonus points if it's one you haven't been to before.) Order a dish you haven't tried before.

Here's the next of *50 Ways to Enjoy Turning Fifty:*

Way #24: Do something creative — just for fun

If you plunk down random objects in front of any toddler, they will try to make things out of them. It's human nature to create. There's something innately engaging and satisfying about making something. Anything. Just for fun.

The problem is that as we get older, we tend to judge what we make — and that just saps the fun out of it. Evaluating or assessing what we create fosters stress and frustration. To the extent you can suspend judgment, however, creative outlets are a heckuva lotta fun. It doesn't matter if you see yourself as an *artiste* or the opposite: You *can* create.

You can slap together random items just for the heck of it. It might be words or foods or computer code or movements or craft supplies or hardware or dollar store finds. You could cook something. Write something. Doodle. Dance in your living room. Make a greeting card. Take some photos. Cut images from magazines and glue them together in a collage. Go to the hardware store or craft store or dollar store to seek cool things to put together in a new way. (If you want more ideas, there's an endless source of inspiration at www.pinterest.com.)

If you choose to, you can use your fiftieth year as an opportunity to create something.

Jean had dabbled in analog photography in his youth. When he turned fifty, he took up digital photography and found a vast online community devoted to his new passion. He had a ball learning new techniques, perfecting his prints, and entering contests.

ACTIVITY:

Make something. Anything. Just for fun. Suspend all judgment.

ACTIVITY:

Go to a store at which you usually don't shop. (E.g., a hardware store, a craft store, a nursery, or a dollar store.) Seek cool things to put together in a new way.

ACTIVITY:

Browse www.pinterest.com. Find something you'd like to make.

Ж

Here's the next of *50 Ways to Enjoy Turning Fifty:*

Way #25: Explore somewhere new

Many people use turning fifty as an excuse to take a trip somewhere they haven't been before. Heidi went to the Galapagos. David enjoyed camping in Death Valley. Bryanne rode her motorcycle through Central America.

Janet gathered other girlfriends who were turning fifty to celebrate together in Croatia.

"Island hopping, sailing, mountain biking along the Dalmatia coast. Rome afterwards for five days," she reported. "Great exercise, spectacular scenery, good company, and some culture thrown in for good measure."

If you can't swing a safari or cruise or other dream vacation, there's nothing stopping you from covering new territory closer to home. What day trips would be interesting or fun for you? What new places could you explore that are reasonably close? Are there parks or facilities or galleries other pockets of your community you could mosey around for an hour or so?

Hazel and Hank bought a walking tour book with the intent of rediscovering their city together. Glenn made it a personal mission to try every hiking trail within an hour of his home. Sarah sussed out the best places to take sunset photographs.

What new places would you like to go during your fiftieth year?

Ж

ACTIVITY:

1. List places near your home that you would like to explore but haven't yet.

    ➢

    ➢

    ➢

    ➢

    ➢

    ➢

    ➢

2. List ten places farther away that you would like to explore but haven't yet. Include at least one "dream destination."

    ➢

    ➢

    ➢

    ➢

    ➢

    ➢

    ➢

    ➢

    ➢

3. Make a point of visiting at least one of these places this year.

Chapter 6

Looking Back

Turning fifty is a natural time to review your life — to reflect on what you've experienced thus far.

Ж

Here's the next of *50 Ways to Enjoy Turning Fifty:*

Way #26: Review your life thus far

Many people find that thinking back on their lives is an enjoyable activity and need no help doing so. If that is true for you, kindly skip ahead to Chapter Seven.

However, if you are hesitant to look back on your life…or if you're not sure how to do so…or if you'd like a more structured approach, this chapter is for you.

If you are hesitant to review your life for fear of re-living unpleasant events or dredging up regrets, consider this: There is much more "good" and "neutral" in your past than "bad."

Regardless of what you've experienced in your life, there are many **benefits** to looking back:

- you will gain a better understanding of who you really are

- you will develop a deeper appreciation of your strengths and preferences

- you will remind yourself what's important to you

- you will re-live your triumphs and accomplishments

- you can reframe unpleasant events in terms of whatever good came out of them — what you learned, who stepped up, how it changed you, how it prepared you for future events, and so forth

- you will re-discover hidden gems — significant people in each chapter of your life

- you will find some nice surprises

- you will gather new ideas to make the most of turning fifty

---

THOUGHT EXPERIMENT:

1. Use the timeline on page 63 to make note of important events in your life:
   - Draw long vertical lines across this timeline to denote the different chapters of your life in a way that's meaningful for you. *(E.g., pre-school, elementary school, high school, college, working, parenting, etc.)*
   - Put X's on the timeline to mark events significant to you. *(E.g., first romance, graduations, major trips, major moves, first job, buying a home, weddings, births of children, getting a pet, losing a loved one, changing jobs, job promotions, etc.)*

2. On pages 64 – 65 are Life Review Questions you can answer about each chapter of your life (i.e. the ones you denoted in question 1). Make enough photocopies of pages 64 and 65 so you can fill them out for each life chapter.

3. Schedule some uninterrupted time for personal reflection. Select one life chapter from your timeline and answer the Life Review Questions.

4. When you have another uninterrupted period of time, focus on a different life chapter and answer the Life Review Questions.

5. Repeat this process until you've worked through every life chapter. Pace yourself gently so you give full and thoughtful attention to each life chapter.

6. Once you begin this process, you are likely to find that, between sessions, other memories pop up — that's great! As new ideas emerge, add them to your answers.

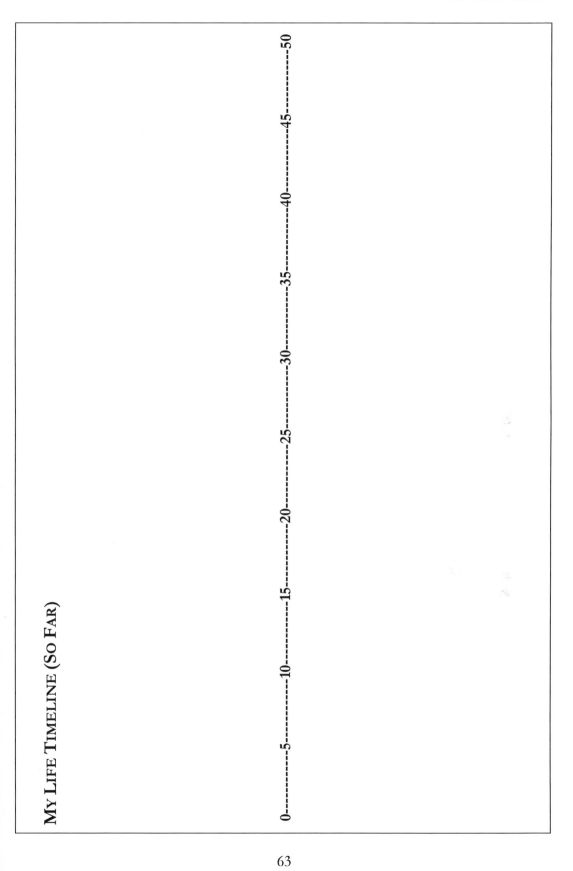

MY LIFE TIMELINE (SO FAR)

0 ----- 5 ----- 10 ----- 15 ----- 20 ----- 25 ----- 30 ----- 35 ----- 40 ----- 45 ----- 50

LIFE REVIEW QUESTIONS - PAGE ONE -

Today I will focus on this Chapter of my Life: _____

1. What do you remember from this period?

2. Who were the key people in your life at this time?

3. Who do you remember fondly from this time period?

4. Where were you? Describe where you lived.

5. What were your chief activities? Amusements? Challenges?

LIFE REVIEW QUESTIONS - PAGE TWO -

6. What were you like at this time? Describe your personality. How did you look?
   How did you dress?

7. What was your chief motivation during this time?

8. What was your chief failing during this time?

9. If you could go back and give yourself messages at that time, what would you say?

ACTIVITY:

After you've worked through all your life chapters, review your notes, then answer the following questions:

1. What recurring themes do you see?

2. What surprises?

3. List five true highlights of your life:

   ➤

   ➤

   ➤

   ➤

   ➤

4. What things did you once love that are no longer part of your life?

5. What new ideas do you have for making your fiftieth year the best ever? (Add them to your plans.)

Chapter 7

Looking Within

What does Barb love about turning fifty? "Finally understanding who I am and living confidently in that," she says.

She's not alone. Turning fifty is a natural time to contemplate who we really are, how we got here, and what's really important to us.

Ж

Here's the next of *50 Ways to Enjoy Turning Fifty:*

Way #27: Identify your true priorities

What's really, truly important to you? Emphasis on *you*. This is not what society says is important. Or what your Dad or your boss or your childhood chum believe should be your top priorities. This is the time to be clear and candid about what matters to *you*.

If Aunt Mabel warns that your bank account is what "should" matter most, but you can list twenty things you care about more, then be true to yourself.

Let's be more specific: What is important to you NOW? These days. In your current life. Not what was important in your twenties or thirties or even last year. Right here and now, what is most meaningful and fulfilling?

Kevin is a successful entrepreneur. Making money has been his top priority for his entire adult life. When he turned fifty, his priorities shifted. Having made his fortune, he realized he was now more interested in putting it to good use, so he started a philanthropic foundation to do just that.

Hazel and Hank turned fifty about the time they became empty-nesters. Whereas their previous priority had been raising their son, they're new focus became their marriage.

"We seem to be having more date nights. It's kind of like starting over," reported Hazel. "Last night we had perogies and sausages at the local Polish festival. We danced to a polka band and enjoyed ourselves a lot!"

KEY QUESTIONS:

1. Think about your present life. What's most important to you these days? What makes life worth living? Be candid.

2. Which activities mean the most to you? Which are the most fulfilling?

3. What objects mean the most? What clues do they give you about what's really, truly important to you?

4. Which concepts do you hold dearest?

5. Now compare your current perspective with the "you" of the past. Scan your Life Review notes — or just reflect back in general. Think back on your life so far:

When you think back on different stages of your life, what's been most important to you?

Of these items, circle what still holds true.

What has changed? What have you outgrown?

6. Think about the future: As you imagine your fifties, sixties, seventies, and beyond, what do you expect will be most important to you? The most fulfilling?

Here's the next of *50 Ways to Enjoy Turning Fifty:*

Way #28: **Reflect on who you really are now**

People grow and change over their lifetime. Who you are at fifty is not who you were at twenty or thirty or forty.

Linda became less uptight and anxious — more calm and flexible — as the years went by. Darren had battled depression and alcoholism during his thirties but he sought treatment in his forties and by the time he was fifty, he was much more centered and grounded. Adrian became interested in spirituality later in life and developed a kinder, gentler persona.

Who are you now?

KEY QUESTIONS:

Answer the following questions as candidly as possible:

1. How would you describe your personality?

2. What are your personal strengths?

3. What are your personal challenges?

---

4. When you think back over the past five decades, how have you changed? How would you describe the shift in yourself from your twenties to your thirties to your forties to now?

5. What five words best describe you today?

> ➤
>
> ➤
>
> ➤
>
> ➤
>
> ➤

It's one thing to look within. It's another to see how you are showing up in the world.

ACTIVITY:

Select at least three significant people in your life. Be prudent in your choice: only survey people you love and trust unconditionally.

Ask each of them for five words that best describe you today.

Here's the next of *50 Ways to Enjoy Turning Fifty:*

Way #29: Examine what your attire says about you

How we present ourselves to the world says a lot about us. Our clothes communicate how we see ourselves. Our personalities and preferences. How well we treat ourselves.

ACTIVITY:

Go to a mirror. Take a look at what you're wearing right now.

- What five words would you use to describe your attire?

- What does your current outfit say about you?

Take a moment to examine each item you are wearing. Assess its quality. How does it fit? To what extent does it suit your personality? How does it make you feel about yourself? When did you acquire it?

If you are pleased with what you are wearing, please skip ahead to Way #30.

If, instead, your attire doesn't look good or feel good, I invite you to read on: You deserve to dress in a way that pleases you. Why not use your fiftieth as an opportunity to re-assess what you wear?

As you select your daily attire, choose garments that fit well and that suit your true personality. Avoid wearing anything that makes you feel icky for any reason. Give special attention to older garments: Do they communicate who you are today? Savor those classic pieces that make you feel great. Jettison anything that does not.

KEY QUESTION:

Think about who you really are today. What do you want to communicate about yourself to anyone who sees you?

ACTIVITIES

1. Put together an attractive outfit that reflects the current you. By "outfit", I mean a complete head-to-toe look: socks, underwear, garments, outerwear, shoes, accessories, hair and, if you desire, makeup. You might have the elements in your closet already…or perhaps you need to create or purchase something new. Think of this as your "birthday ensemble" or, dare I say it, your "birthday suit."

2. Find an opportunity to wear your birthday ensemble.

Another element here: treating yourself well, with respect. How well do your clothes fit? Are there items in your closet that are unflattering or in need of repair? Case in point: Does your underwear need upgrading?

ACTIVITIES:

1. Go through your wardrobe, piece by piece. Remove anything that does not reflect the real you. Eliminate anything that is unflattering, that doesn't fit, or that needs mending. Donate, sell, fix, or toss these items.

2. Treat yourself to new socks and underwear.

Ж

Here's the next of *50 Ways to Enjoy Turning Fifty:*

Way #30: Appreciate yourself

Words are one of the most powerful things I know. They can soothe and wound. They can delight and destroy. They can entertain and transform.

The most powerful words are the ones we use to describe ourselves. We might not even be aware of what those words are — or where they came from.

The following activity is a powerful one adapted from *Vein of Gold* by Julia Cameron. In it you will consider the words that other people have labeled you in the past. These words can shape how we think about ourselves. For example, maybe when you were a kid, someone called you "scattered" or "bossy." Maybe it hurt. Perhaps you laughed. Either way, you may have inadvertently internalized the label.

This activity is meant to check what self-labels you have inside…and then to process them accordingly. If something stings, there is an opportunity to examine it. Question the validity of any hurtful or negative label. It might not be true. It might not be accurate. It was just that person's opinion at that time — and probably said more about their issues and personality than it did about you.

The next step is to convert any negative label into a more helpful, more accurate one. For example "scattered" could be re-written as "interested in many things." "Bossy" could be re-written as "strong."

When I did this exercise, it triggered a clear memory of the occasion when an elementary school chum expressed her exasperation that I "start all these different projects and never finish any of them!" She called me a "flake." It hurt. This unexpected recollection revealed a negative label that, to my surprise, I'd been carrying deep inside for four decades.

As soon as I identified it, I could question its validity. The truth is that sure I was involved in a lot of activities as a kid. Yes, I started many different projects. However I finished many of them. (And what did my projects have to do with her? Why was she so bothered by them?) The cosmic Truth is that no one *has* to finish *everything* they start. In fact, the physical reality is that it's absolutely impossible to do so.

Okay, my school chum thought I was a flake (and probably still does), but that label isn't accurate. I'm not a flake. I'm quite conscientious and responsible. However, I do have a lot going on. I do start a lot of projects. Some don't get finished. A more accurate label would be that I'm "interested in many things." It's true! I am interested in many things! I'll shout it proudly!

It was helpful to identify the negative label I'd unwittingly internalized. It was satisfying indeed to exorcise it and to transform it into a more helpful, pleasant description. I invite you to do the same.

On the following page is a structured exercise so you can identify any negative labels you recall from your youth. If something "pinches", write it down. (If you get stuck, ask: What are the worst things I was called as a kid?) Next, you'll do a reality check. To what extent was this label accurate? You'll conclude by re-writing it into words or phrases that are more accurate and helpful.

ЖK

THOUGHT EXPERIMENT: REWRITE LABELS

Write down some negative labels you recall from childhood (*e.g., bossy*)	Is this true? Is this accurate? What evidence is there to the contrary?	Convert these negative words into more helpful, accurate interpretations (*e.g., strong*)

ACTIVITY:

Post your more helpful, accurate labels somewhere where you will see them often.
E.g., on a Post-It in your planner or wallet; in your phone, tablet, or computer.

Here's the next of *50 Ways to Enjoy Turning Fifty:*

Way #31: Examine your thinking

What do you spend time thinking about? What occupies your mind during the day?

When I asked myself these questions, I was embarrassed. Much as I would like to believe that I spend my days contemplating world events or the meaning of life or dozens of other, more substantial topics, the truth is, I don't.

I verified this by spending a few days paying attention to whatever was on my mind. The sad reality was that that few great, weighty topics drifted across my consciousness. Shockingly little occupied my mind, other than my day's "to do's." Little thought was spent on The Big Picture. There was only minimal brainstorming about cool, creative projects.

"I'm wasting my brain," I concluded. "I'm frittering away my life, futzing over inconsequential matters." I became keenly motivated to change the situation. Which brought me to an important question: What would I *like* to be thinking about? On what would I prefer to be spending my mental energy?

What a big impact this small shift in focus can have.

When David examined his thinking, he was shocked at the amount of his negative self-talk. (*"I'm an idiot!"* *"Way to go, loser. This is crap."*) He hadn't realized how much time he spent berating himself needlessly. Once he realized what he was doing, he could recognize it — even laugh at himself for doing it (*"Ha! There goes my inner bully"*) — and shift to more positive internal dialogue. (*"It's just a mistake, not the end of the world."* *"This is plenty good enough."*)

THOUGHT EXPERIMENT:

1. Quick! What are you thinking about? What's on your mind right now? Write it down.

---

2. What would you like to be thinking about? On what would you prefer to be spending your mental energy?

3. Keep your list handy, somewhere you will see often. (E.g., an electronic note in your phone, or computer. A list posted inside your medicine cabinet.)

ACTIVITY:

At random times this week, stop and identify what you're thinking about. Remind yourself about what you would prefer to be thinking.

Here's the next of *50 Ways to Enjoy Turning Fifty:*

Way #32: Examine any unfulfilled life dreams

Most of us have Life Dreams at different phases in life — particular things we'd like to do or accomplish during our lives.

Some of these we do. Some, we don't.

Of the latter, sometimes we outgrow our dreams. Maybe as a teen, you aspired to be a rock star…and now, at fifty, you're content to avoid the musical limelight. It could be that in your twenties you dreamed of climbing Everest someday…but now that arduous trek appeals less.

Other unfulfilled dreams don't go away. They niggle at the back of our minds for decades. Maybe you always wanted to visit Paris. Or publish a book. Or get a bachelor's degree. Or learn to tap dance. Or build an adobe house.

It's up to you to decide how important your unfulfilled dreams are. Not how doable or practical they are — how *important* are they. To *you.*

If you have any important unfulfilled dreams, guess what? You're turning fifty. If you don't tackle them now, then when will you? Take that trip. Write that novel. Sign up for that class. *It's Only 'Too Late' if You Don't Start Now.* (If you'd like more on this topic, Barbara Sher's book by that title is highly recommended.)

Laura Ingalls Wilder began writing a newspaper column in her forties. She didn't write or publish her *Little House* series until she was in her sixties.

Julian Fellowes wrote his first screenplay at the age of fifty. It was entitled *Gosford Park* and it won the Academy Award for Best Original Screenplay. His subsequent scripts? The Emmy-award winning television series *Downton Abbey.* Are we glad he didn't think it was "too late" for him to start writing screenplays?

Diana Nyad was twenty-nine the first time she attempted to swim from Cuba to Florida without a protective cage. She didn't make it. When she turned sixty, her dream rekindled and she resumed her quest. It took untold hours of training and preparation. She underwent four more arduous crossings until she finally succeeded, in her fifth attempt, at age sixty-four. She was the first — and, to date, only — person to ever accomplish this feat.

Colonel Harland Sanders was sixty-five years old when he launched his Kentucky Fried Chicken (KFC) restaurants.

Peter Mark Roget didn't start compiling his Thesaurus until he was seventy. It was first published when he was seventy-three.

Grandma Moses began painting when she was seventy-six. She created more than 1600 canvasses over the next three decades.

THOUGHT EXPERIMENT:

1. As you reflect back on your life, what have been your Big Dreams at different stages of life? Make a list.

2. Review your list. Put a great big checkmark beside those items you actually did. Congratulate yourself for your accomplishments.

continued →

3. Now, consider each unfulfilled Big Dream, one at a time. Decide if it is still important to you.

For unfulfilled dreams that are no longer important to you: Let them go.

For unfulfilled dreams that are important, ask yourself: What actions can I take to move forward on this?

Some dreams might require modification. Rather than scaling the deadly Everest, how about the easier Kilimanjaro? Or a mountain closer to home? Or maybe you just want to spend more time hiking?

Some Life Dreams may seem impossible or impractical at this juncture. If it still feels important to you, then ask yourself what might be a reasonable substitute. What would be a similar experience that is possible now? For example, if your Life Dream was to be a professional dancer, but it's not physically possible now, what is? You could take dance classes — or teach them. You could get into Zumba. You could organize a dance showcase. You could go out dancing with friends.

What aspects or elements of your Life Dream can you experience?

KEY QUESTION:

What modified versions of your Life Dream(s) are possible?

Chapter 8

Expressing Gratitude

When we turn fifty, we have a lot to appreciate. This milestone birthday provides an opportunity to be truly thankful for what we've experienced along the way.

Ж

Here's the next of *50 Ways to Enjoy Turning Fifty:*

Way #33: Express appreciation for aspects of your life

Reflect on your life thus far. For what are you grateful? Consider all areas of your life. What experiences have enriched your life? Which relationships?

KEY QUESTIONS:

Reflect on your life. For what are you thankful? For what are you grateful?

ACTIVITY:

Set a timer for ten minutes. See how many ways you can complete these sentences before the buzzer goes:

I'm grateful for

I'm grateful that

I'm grateful

I'm grateful I've

I'm thankful for

I've thankful that

I'm thankful

I'm thankful I've

I appreciate

I so appreciate

I'm so grateful for

I'm so grateful that

I'm so grateful

I'm so grateful I've

I'm so thankful for

I've so thankful that

I'm so thankful

I'm so thankful I've

My life is rich and full because

It's easy to express gratitude for happy occasions. More difficult events can be more challenging to appreciate, however.

One of my professional heroes is M.J. Ryan, author of *Attitude of Gratitude* — a seminal book on the topic. She contributed a wonderful story to my co-authored *Happiness* book that demonstrated "blessings in disguise." The punch line: Some gifts come wrapped in sandpaper.

Take Louisa, for example. She underwent simple day surgery and things went horribly wrong. She went into anaphylactic shock and almost died. Doesn't sound like much of a gift or blessing, does it? But when Louisa unwrapped the metaphorical sandpaper, she found plenty.

"Well this experience certainly did wake me up," she wrote me recently. "I am no longer complacent or bored. I am grateful for the people in my life and mindful of how I treat people. Normally we keep birthdays pretty quiet. I decided then and there that I was never taking another birthday for granted. We had thirty-five people here to help me celebrate my fiftieth last July. I joined the gym, and am getting very active. I'm enjoying life and renewing old friendships and nurturing the existing ones. I just joined a yoga class and am going to sign up for conversational Italian. I am aiming to be fluent enough for a future trip to Italy."

Now you needn't wait for a matter of life and death to be grateful or to express gratitude for all that's in your life. Turning fifty is a natural time to reflect on your life — and to express appreciation for it.

KEY QUESTIONS:

Think about a difficult time you've experienced. Were there any silver linings? Any lessons learned? What "blessings" arose from those situations?

Here's the next of *50 Ways to Enjoy Turning Fifty:*

Way #34: Express gratitude to significant people in your life

Who have been the greatest positive influences on your life, personally and professionally? Who has supported you? Who has inspired you? Do they know how important or meaningful they have been to you?

One pleasure of turning fifty is that it is an opportunity to identify and appreciate those people who have enhanced our first five decades.

When Mari turned fifty, she invited ten female friends to a luncheon to honor "significant women in her life." Over sparkling wine and a light salad meal, she gave a short speech to explain why each guest was there. Mari noted the commonalities among them — how the threads of their lives had woven together.

How was the event?

"It was such fun," reported Mari, "I've decided I'll gather this group together again next year!"

It's one thing to know that you are grateful for significant people in your life. It's another thing to actually inform them of your appreciation. No person on the planet hears "thank you" too much. No one is "sick and tired" of being appreciated. Saying "thank you" to someone is always worthwhile.

When I was a kid, I wrote a fan letter to author Margaret Atwood. To my surprise and delight, she replied! She wrote, "On an off day, a letter like yours is certainly a quick pick-me-up. I am of course delighted that you enjoyed my books so much…" and went on to wish me well with my own writing. Just think: My note was a "quick pick-me-up" to an author who has enriched my life!

Now this was during a time when people actually wrote letters. On paper. Today, thanks to the internet and social media, it's now much easier to communicate appreciation to people we admire. Whenever I read a book I enjoy, for example, I do my best to contact the author online to praise their work.

Ditto for my career role models — Martha Beck (*Finding Your Own North Star, The Joy Diet*); Barbara Sher (*I Could Do Anything if Only I Knew What It Was, Life the Life You Love*); Susan Jeffers (*Feel the Fear and Do it Anyway, Embracing Uncertainty*); and M.J. Ryan (*Attitudes of Gratitude, This Year I Will…*). I've had the honor of corresponding with them…and actually collaborating with the latter two on a book.

I've used the same method to reach out to personal heroes — like Mollie Katzen — author of many seminal vegetarian cookbooks beginning with *The Moosewood Cookbook* (a.k.a. the Vegetarian Bible). I'm grateful indeed to have had Mollie Katzen's recipes enhancing my culinary repertoire for the past decades. It is a personal thrill to communicate with her now via social media — to thank her directly.

Then there are the most significant people of all: the childhood chums I cherish. When my mother passed away, my friends rolled up their sleeves to help me deal with all that needed to be done. It was the most challenging thing I've ever faced and I could not have made it through without my friends' kind, generous, support.

To whom would you like to express your appreciation?

THOUGHT EXPERIMENT:	
List significant people in your life. *This might include people you actually know as well as personal or professional heroes.*	For what would you like to thank them? How can you express your appreciation to this person?

ACTIVITY: Express appreciation to the significant people in your life. If you can't tell them in person, write them, email them, or reach out through social media.

Here's the next of *50 Ways to Enjoy Turning Fifty:*

Way #35: Express daily thanks

It doesn't matter what's going on in our lives — there's always *something* for which we can be grateful. We're breathing. We have water to drink. We have food and shelter. We have functioning brains. It's a powerful practice to express gratitude for what we have, who we are, and what we experience. It casts our lives in a more positive light. It shifts our focus to what's working well, rather than what's not.

Daily gratitude begets more of what we love in life. The more we appreciate certain aspects of life, the more we foster them.

Sometimes people try this practice and before long it devolves into a rote daily practice akin to writing out a shopping list. If you've tried this practice and found it lacking, do what Einstein did: Rather than just listing the things for which you are grateful, write out the reason why.

This small alteration — the additional explanation of *why* we're grateful — elevates and deepens each item exponentially. Rather than jotting down "my home office" on a laundry list of bullet points, it's much more powerful to specify the reasons. (*"I'm grateful for my home office because it's comfortable and well organized and pleasingly decorated and full of books I adore plus it provides a pleasant, quiet space to accomplish my work efficiently and effectively."*)

I could list dozens of jaw-dropping stories about the power of the practice of expressing daily gratitude…yet the best possible examples are from your own experience. Do yourself a favor: Try the next activity and witness the consequences.

ACTIVITY:

Every day for the next week, write down at least five things for which you're grateful — and specify why.

"I'm grateful for X because…"

"I'm so thankful for Y because…"

Aim for at least five different items every day. Watch what happens.

Ж

Chapter 9

Putting Things in Order

Given everything there is to do in a given week, it's easy to put off those things that are important but not necessarily urgent. Things like updating your will or reviewing your finances or even revamping your living space. Milestone birthdays provide a great opportunity to put things in order. Why not use your fiftieth as an opportunity to take care of what's important in your life?

Ж

Here's the next of *50 Ways to Enjoy Turning Fifty:*

> ## Way #36: Identify important things in your life requiring stewardship

"Stewardship" is a stodgy sounding word yet a wonderful concept: Stewardship means taking good and thoughtful care of something. It's a warmer, cozier, more competent way of approaching the many responsibilities in your life. Rather than thinking "Oh crap, I have to do X, Y, and Z!" it's a shift to calmly managing whatever comes up for the purpose of taking good care of what's important in your life.

Please turn to the next page to take stock. Of what — or whom — do you want to be taking good care? Your relationships — personal and professional? Your home? Your family? Your career? Your finances? Something else? Answer thoughtfully and candidly.

Next consider how you might take better care of this person or thing. If anything seems like a burden, how might you reframe it into more positive terms?

For example, if your domestic responsibilities seem overwhelming, it might help to reframe your chores as taking good care of your home. "Ugh. I have to clean the kitchen. Again." becomes "I'm making my household cleaner and safer" or "I'm taking good care of my household members." If financial tasks make you squeamish or avoidant, try approaching them as "taking good care of my money."

KEY QUESTIONS:		
Of what — or whom — do you want to be taking good care?	How can you take better care of this person or thing?	Does this seem like a burden? How might you reframe it into more positive terms?

Here's the next of *50 Ways to Enjoy Turning Fifty:*

Way #37: Put your finances in order

When Irene's husband surprised her with a request for a divorce after twenty years of marriage, she was stunned. Besides the emotional and social upheaval, she found herself in a financial mess. Her spouse had taken care of all their finances throughout her marriage. She didn't know where their accounts and assets were, let alone practicalities like passwords. She was essentially destitute and entirely at the mercy of a person intent on cutting her out of his life.

Karl was in a similar bind when his wife died unexpectedly. She had been their household's financial manager…and he had a helluva time convincing credit card companies, financial institutions, and service providers to allow him access to their accounts.

"The phone company would not allow me to even make inquiries into our account because my name wasn't on it," he said. "It was a costly, stressful, time-consuming mess to sort everything out."

ACTIVITY:

If you have a domestic partner, do this together: Make a list of all your household's financial accounts and service providers as well as how to access them.

To the extent possible, put both of your names on every account.

Keep this list in a safe, secure location and update it with any changes, as they occur.

Once you have your basic financial practicalities in hand, it's time to look at your financial plans more broadly. What is your current financial situation? What is your monthly income? How much do you spend? How much do you save? If you don't know, it's pretty much impossible to manage your finances effectively.

ACTIVITY:

Clear two uninterrupted hours. Review and analyze your most recent financial statements. Look at your past few months' bank statements, investments, credit card bills, and your regular recurring bills. Determine your average monthly income and expenditures.

Once you've surveyed your current finances, identify your fiscal goals: What do you want to do with your money? Get out of debt? Save for something in particular? Create financial freedom? Sock away cash for retirement? Donate to good causes? Educate yourself about investments? Be very specific. What is most pressing? What is most important to you?

KEY QUESTIONS:

1. Based on your analysis of your recent finances, what are your key financial goal(s)?

2. If you have several financial goals, prioritize them.

3. Focus on your top financial goal. How will you reach it? What needs to happen? Make a plan.

Here's the next of *50 Ways to Enjoy Turning Fifty:*

Way #38: Put your legal paperwork in order

When my mother passed away unexpectedly, the greatest gift she gave me was that her legal paperwork was accurate, complete, and up to date. Her wishes were crystal clear. It's hard to think straight when you're grieving, so having everything spelled out was a relief. Having all the paperwork in order also saved me the expense, stress, and emotional toll of probate, legal wrangling, and tax hell.

Julia was not so fortunate. Sorting out her mother's estate required a year of hemorrhaging money for legal fees and taxes — plus grappling with a mountain of indecipherable paperwork and umpteen stressful meetings.

"It was so emotionally draining," she said. "Every meeting with the lawyer meant we had to re-live Mom's death. A half hour probate meeting would knock me out for the rest of the day."

Sid had it worse: When his parents died, the surviving family members squabbled over the estate.

"I can't believe it happened in my own family," he lamented. "It was so unpleasant and such a cliché. It was so bad I haven't spoken to my own sister in five years."

Two points here: First, your milestone presents an opportunity to ensure that your parents' legal paperwork is in order and that you understand their wishes. Who do they want making medical decisions for them? Who do they want making financial decisions for them? Do they have a will? Who do they want to manage their estate? Do they have any specific bequests? Where are their key legal and financial documents?

Second, consider your own situation. What kind of experience do you want for the people you care about?

Yes this can be a morbid, scary topic. Yes, you're "only" fifty. Yet it behooves you to put things in order for the people important to you.

If you haven't already, now is the time to update your will, your medical wishes, your funerary wishes, and all other legal documents. It's also helpful to document your financial holdings, to bundle important information with your legal documents, and to place it all in a safe, secure location.

ACTIVITY:

1. To what extent do you know your parents' wishes?
   - Who do they want making medical decisions for them? Under what circumstances?
   - Who do they want making financial decisions for them? Under what circumstances?
   - Do they have a will?
   - Who do they want managing their estate, should something happen to them?
   - Do they have any specific bequests?
   - What are their funerary wishes?
   - Where are their key documents?

2. As appropriate, have conversations with your parents and key family members to ensure that you understand their wishes.

ACTIVITY:

1. Review your legal documents including your will, your medical wishes, and your funerary wishes.

2. What's in place already?

3. What gaps need to be addressed?

4. Take the necessary steps to ensure all your legal documents are accurate and complete.

5. Inform your executor(s) of your medical and funerary wishes.

6. Should something happen to you, what information will your heirs need? Make a detailed record of important legal and financial information such as financial holdings, passwords, etc.

7. Place your important legal and financial documents in a safe, secure place. Inform your executor(s) of their location.

Ж

Here's the next of *50 Ways to Enjoy Turning Fifty:*

Way #39: **Put your living space in order**

Unless you're a neatnik or are in the process of selling your home, odds are your living space could use some attention. Rare is the person who has a perfectly functioning, perfectly organized, perfectly beautiful abode. If you choose to do so, you can use your fiftieth as an opportunity to improve your living space.

Steve's living room was a vivid crimson homage to the 1980's — until he used his milestone year as an excuse to redecorate. Abby redid her kitchen. Earl purchased a long-coveted Eames lounge chair.

ACTIVITY:

1. Walk around your living space with paper and pen (or tablet). In each room or area, ask yourself the following questions:

   - What's working well for you in this space?

   - What's not?

   - What looks good?

   - What doesn't?

   - What needs attention or repair?

2. After you've surveyed your space, review your notes. What would you really like to address this year? Make a list.

3. Circle your number one priority.

4. What's the simplest, easiest thing you could do to move forward on your top priority?

5. Do it. Take action to improve your living space.

Chapter 10

Eliminating What You Don't Need

When we turn fifty, we're at a point in life at which we can release those things that no longer serve us. Whether it's past regrets or grudges or excess belongings or bad habits, now is a great time to let them go. Release old baggage. Clear the decks to better enjoy the decades to come.

Here's the next of *50 Ways to Enjoy Turning Fifty:*

Way #40: Prune your belongings

You might not be a pack-rat. Your living and working spaces may be free of clutter. But look around and see what excessive objects are occupying your space. What are you holding onto that you don't really need?

There is some kind of supernatural process by which stuff accumulates. I sure don't need everything I own and I bet the same is true for you. For example: Are you holding on to supplies you might need "someday" but haven't touched in years? Have you been lugging around books that really aren't that important to you? Does your closet hold items that don't fit or don't flatter or don't get worn in your present life? Are you hanging onto items others have given you that you don't really need or want…but you feel guilty about getting rid of them?

My mother was a shopper. Also a "collector." It was eye-opening indeed to clean out her house after she passed away. When you are forced to go through all of someone else's stuff, you realize that's all it is: stuff. (If you haven't seen the George Carlin comedy routine about "Stuff" in a while, check it out. There's no better indictment of how chained we can become to our belongings.)

Going through my mother's possessions gave me fresh eyes when I looked at my own things. Even though I'm not a clutterer, I became better able to see what I have that I don't need — and to take action accordingly. It became easy to winnow books, to prune my closet, and to donate art supplies to others. Doing so felt freeing and fabulous. I was delighted to pass on objects to others who were more likely to use them. I was tickled to clear space in my office and my home.

Fifty is at terrific time to let go of:

- things you don't need

- things you don't like

- things you aren't using

- things that make you feel guilty or otherwise icky

- things you're holding onto because they might be useful "someday"

- things that need repair — that you are unlikely to fix

- clothes that don't fit or aren't flattering

- things you want to give to someone "someday." Why not give them now?

Give yourself a gift by jettisoning your excess belongings. The less you hang onto, the more space and freedom you'll have. And the more your living space will reflect the current "you."

Only hold onto:

- things you love

- things that make you feel good

- things you use

- things in good repair (or that you commit to repair within the next month)

- things that fit you well and look good on you

ACTIVITY:

Obtain three cardboard boxes. Mark one "donate", one "give", and one "sell." Put them beside a large garbage can.

Now: Walk around your living space. Find at least ten items that belong in these receptacles. Distribute them accordingly.

ACTIVITY:

1. Pick the easiest possible space to purge — a sock drawer, a cupboard, the bathroom, wherever. Remove all the contents. As you do so, get rid of what you don't need. Give it away, throw it away, sell it — do what makes sense to get it out of your space. If in doubt, you don't need it. It's just "stuff." When you put the remaining items back, organize them neatly.

2. Make a list of the rooms or areas of your living space.

3. On another occasion, repeat the first activity, focusing on a different room or area.

4. Repeat this process until you've worked your way through your list. *Maybe you tackle one room a month or one drawer or cupboard per week — find a schedule that works for you so that you can go through your entire living space this year. Jettison what you don't need.*

5. Set up an ongoing system by which you will keep clutter at bay. *(Heidi, for example, has a "one in - one out" rule. If she buys something new, she gets rid of something old. James makes a regular practice of pruning his belongings throughout the year. Pat schedules an annual spring cleaning/purge to go through the family's entire living space.)* What will work for you?

If you are still not convinced of the benefits of decluttering your living space, consider your family: It is a horrible thing to have to go through someone else's belongings. The more you hold onto, the more difficult and unpleasant you are making it for those you leave behind. The more you hold onto, the harder it is for others to detect what is valuable and what is sentimentally important.

Ж

Here's the next of *50 Ways to Enjoy Turning Fifty:*

Way #41: Break an unhelpful or unhealthy habit

We all do things that aren't particularly helpful or healthy. Maybe we gossip or overspend or wallow in negative thoughts. When Karen turned fifty, she realized she wanted to reduce her alcohol consumption. As someone who is "interested in many things", I used to spend way too much time surfing the internet. At fifty, Phil's metabolism would no longer allow him to munch on potato chips every single night without unflattering repercussions.

What are *your* vices? What habits do you have that aren't particularly healthy or helpful?

KEY QUESTIONS:

1. What one habit would you most like to cease? (If in doubt, pick the activity you're most embarrassed about.)

2. To what extent do you want to overcome this habit?

3. Will you commit to make a change?

If you resolve to reduce or eliminate this unwanted behavior, please read on.

However if you're not yet ready, then please move ahead to Way #42 (page 105). Until you decide you really want to change, it's pretty much impossible to overcome an unhealthy or bad habit.

Assuming you're ready to give it a go — to use turning fifty as an opportunity to overcome an unhelpful or unhealthy habit— here's how:

1. Choose a specific goal

Be very clear about what it is you want to accomplish. Rather than saying "I'd like to watch less television", be more concrete and specific. For example: "I intend to watch a maximum of seven hours of TV per week" or "I intend to keep the TV off all day until after dinner" or "No TV during meals" or "I hereby declare Fridays will be TV-free" or whatever it is you want to achieve.

My specific goal is:

2. Make a list of the benefits of changing

What will be the consequences of curtailing your bad habit? Make a list. Review this list at least once a day, every day. Refer to this list if you're tempted to indulge in your unwanted behavior.

List the benefits of curtailing your bad habit:

3. List the costs of not changing

Chronicle the negatives so you have vivid images to bolster what you're trying to do. Again, it's helpful to make a list of the consequences of your bad habit and to review it intermittently.

List the costs and consequences of not curtailing this habit:

4. Find support

Tell supportive friends and family members about the change you are implementing. Who can you truly trust to support you? Ask them for help. Be specific about what you need from them.

Are there particular people you can contact when you feel tempted to backslide? Is there a coach or a mentor who can guide you through the process of overcoming your bad habit?

Are there support groups available you could join? It's very, very helpful to connect with other people going through the same challenges.

Is there someone with whom you could partner up to make the change? Either someone going through the same transition (e.g., you're both committed to stop smoking) or someone going through their own change (e.g., you're cutting down on internet surfing while they are cutting down their junk food intake)?

Are there books that could help? For example, my book *You Can Change Your Life* is a workbook designed to accomplish whatever change you choose. It can be used as a stand-alone guide or as a companion with other books or programs.

```
List possible sources of support:



```

5. Remove temptation

Find ways to make it easy on yourself. Physically remove items from your environment that trigger, facilitate, or enable your unwanted behavior. For example, if you're dieting, remove unhealthy and "trigger" foods from your home. To reduce my internet surfing, I unplug my connection as much as possible during workdays and made it a rule to stay offline on the weekends.

Develop strategies for avoiding temptations in different situations. For example, if you've decided to lay off the booze, how can you navigate social events at which alcohol will be served? Who can support you? Who would you be wise to avoid? What non-alcoholic beverages will you choose to have instead?

Make a list. How can you reduce or avoid temptation?

6. Choose a course of action

Option (a): Cold Turkey

Simply cease your bad habit.

Think about how you'd rather be operating. (For example, let's say you'd like to avoid snacking between meals.) Establish a clear picture of the behavioral pattern you'd prefer and commit yourself to those actions. (For example, choose standard meal times and avoid eating except at those times.)

Option (b): Join an Established Program – and Follow it

Whether it's WeightWatchers or a 12 Step Program, there is likely to be a comprehensive program devoted to curtailing your unwanted habit. This may involve group meetings plus daily activities including reading, journaling, and making a phone commitment to a specific person.

Option (c): Create your Own Personal Program

Decide exactly what you want to do (and not do). What daily activities will keep you on track? (E.g., inspirational reading, journaling, reviewing your costs and benefits lists, checking in with a supportive person, etc.) To whom can you make yourself accountable? (E.g., a coach, friend, or habit-busting buddy.)

Option (d): Wean Yourself via Baby Steps

Begin by measuring and monitoring your normal behavior for a week.

On the following week, keep measuring and monitoring…but this time, impose a limit of 10% less than you did last week. If you are successful for the week, then further reduce your negative activity by another 10 %…and so on until you achieve your ideal activity level.

Circle the option you prefer.

7. Monitor and reward your progress

However you proceed, it's important to chronicle your progress and to reward yourself for every day you follow your game plan.

Recognize that each day you succeed will make future successful days easily and more likely.

Reward yourself for milestones – especially your first day, first week, and first month. Give yourself bonuses for overcoming particular challenges or cravings.

How can you monitor your progress? How can you keep yourself on track? *Consider what you wrote on page 30.*

How would you like to reward yourself for your progress?

What milestones will you seek? How can you reward yourself for reaching them?

8. Forgive yourself for setbacks.

If you revert back to your old ways, forgive yourself and get right back on track. You're human, i.e. imperfect. Do the best you can and carry on.

If you get really stuck, ask yourself, what's really going on here? Dig deeper: What unhealthy, unhelpful beliefs are interfering with your goals?

9. Focus on the big picture.

Look at the overall pattern of progress, rather than focusing on any specific day. *"Well, I didn't do so well today but I stayed on track for the rest of the week…and I'm doing much better this week than last week."*

Here's the next of *50 Ways to Enjoy Turning Fifty:*

Way #42: **Let go of regrets, disappointments, and other old baggage**

When she turned fifty, Barb was thrilled to realize that a lot of what used to bother her no longer affected her.

Are there things in your past you need to release? Regrets or disappointments or past hurts? Imagine how much better you'd feel if you'd get over what happened and move on with your life. Why not make this the year to let go of old baggage?

The following is a guided process to work through past regrets, disappointments, and old baggage. It's most effective when you can clear some uninterrupted time to give your full and thoughtful attention to the questions.

THOUGHT EXPERIMENT:

1. Clear some uninterrupted time. Write down anything from your past that still bothers you. List any of the following that are presently a burden for you:

- unresolved regrets

- disappointments

- missed opportunities

- past perceived "mistakes"

- past hurts

continued →

- "if only's"

- unhelpful or unhealthy thoughts

- unhelpful or unhealthy beliefs

2. Review your list. Circle the item that affects you most. Dispute it in detail. What is the truth? Try a reality check. *For example: "I regret I didn't finish my college degree" might be more helpfully stated as "School was a lower priority than other things at the time. My path was different but I've learned a lot along the way. If I wanted to, I could take classes now. If it's truly important to me, I could work towards a degree. I've seen news articles about people in their eighties and nineties who do just that."* Write out your detailed refutation here.

3. With this item in mind, ask yourself the following:

- What did I learn?

- What good came out of this?

- What positive action can I take now?

THOUGHT EXPERIMENT:

1. Write down something for which you need to forgive yourself.

2. With this in mind, answer the following:

   - What does it cost you to carry this burden?

   - What benefits would there be to forgiving yourself? How would you feel? How would it change how you are living your life?

   - To what extent were you doing the best you could, given the skills, knowledge, and experience you had at the time? To what extent did you learn from it?

   - To what extent can you change what happened?

   - What's stopping you from forgiving yourself?

   - What can you do to forgive yourself?

3. Take a moment. Acknowledge that you are a fallible human, that you make mistakes, and that you deserve forgiveness for them. View yourself with compassion and kindness. Forgive yourself.

(If you'd like to delve more into this topic, there's more in my book, *Get Over It: Overcome Regret, Disappointment and Past Mistakes*.)

Here's the next of *50 Ways to Enjoy Turning Fifty:*

Way #43: Eliminate grudges and conflicts

My best childhood buddy broke off our friendship during high school. I don't know why. At that time, I was too hurt and immature to ask. We remained estranged for the next thirty years. It felt awful anytime I thought about her or the close friendship we once shared.

Through social media, I received word that she was in Illinois battling serious cancer. I contacted her and, to my immense relief, we reconciled. The burden of our history was lifted, replaced by a new affection.

She passed away within a month. It was a heart-breaking event...yet I was so grateful that we reconciled before she died.

There's no need to wait for health crises to repair relationships or address past hurts.

As you think about your relationships with others, do you have any conflicts that need resolving? Are there any past incidents requiring forgiveness? Why not use your fiftieth year as an opportunity to find peace, make amends, and let go of grudges.

THOUGHT EXPERIMENT:	
Make a list of the people with whom you have a current or past unresolved conflict.	For each person, jot down one thing you could do to improve things between you. *This might include small shifts in attitude, words, or thoughts you have about them.*

Regardless of how kind we try to be, each of us have been hurt by someone else — and each of us has hurt someone else. Just as we must apologize and ask forgiveness when we do wrong, it's only fair that we forgive those who wrong us.

Sometimes that's not easy. When someone hurts us, there is a natural resistance to responding with kindness. But forgiveness is not approval for what occurred. Forgiveness is not "letting someone off the hook." Forgiveness is an acknowledgment that we all make mistakes.

"But you don't understand," you may protest. "They were wrong! They hurt me badly! Why should I forgive them?" Well, ask yourself this: Would you rather be right or would you rather be healed? If you want to heal, you must forgive them.

Truthfully, forgiveness is letting YOU off the hook: It's a way to release the pain, the anger, the fear, and the resentment you experience when someone hurts you. Forgiveness gives you the opportunity to heal and move on.

The alternatives don't work. Lashing back or seeking revenge is never as satisfying as you imagine. Harsh actions injure you in the long run. Holding grudges and hard feelings against those who have harmed you hurts you much, much more than it affects them.

The longer you let resentments and regrets fester, the more you are damaging your own peace of mind. It's impossible to be happy if you are bearing burdens from the past. Who does it serve if you are walking around, bitter and seething about something that happened a decade ago…while the person who hurt you can't even remember your name, let alone the incident? Grudges hurt you, not them.

"But it's too late," you may say. No, it isn't. When you hurt someone, it's better to apologize immediately — but it's better to apologize late than not at all. Forgiveness works the same way. You can be way overdue when it comes to forgiving others. But as soon as you do, you can heal. Besides: You can't move forward until you forgive.

"But I don't even know where they are, what they're doing, if they are even alive," you might counter. It doesn't matter. If you can forgive someone in person, it's powerful. But you can also forgive someone without them knowing anything about it. It doesn't matter where they are or what they're doing — you have the power to forgive them, right here, right now.

Forgiveness is really a gift you give yourself. You'll feel the difference in your own heart when you truly forgive someone. There's a little shift, deep down. It feels like relief. It's the first step to replacing the pain of the incident with peace and joy.

Let's review. Think of a specific time in which you were wronged. Someone did a bad thing. Now what are you going to do about it?

Option 1: You can stew — keep it all inside, festering. This only hurts you.

Option 2: You can play the victim. You tell everyone what a horrible thing happened to you and broadcast what a terrible person the perpetrator of the incident is. This only foments negativity and spreads the pain.

Option 3: You can lash back — seek revenge or payback. This may give you momentary satisfaction but it won't feel nearly as satisfying as you anticipate — and it will not heal your pain.

Option 4: You can forgive them and move on. If you want to heal, forgiveness is the answer.

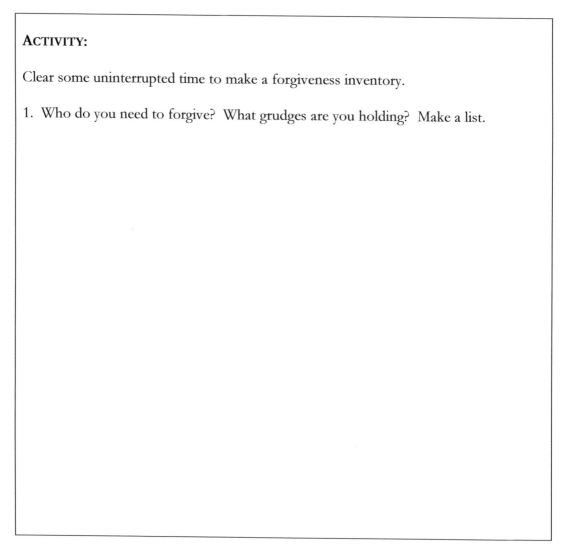

ACTIVITY:

Clear some uninterrupted time to make a forgiveness inventory.

1. Who do you need to forgive? What grudges are you holding? Make a list.

2. Pick one person on your list. Answer the following questions:

- What is it costing you to hold these resentments?

- How does it make you feel?

- How does it affect how you are living your life?

- What benefits might there be to forgiving them? How would you feel? How might it improve your life?

- To what extent were they doing the best they could, given the skills, knowledge, and experience they had at the time?

3. Imagine this person as a child, helpless and alone. Could you have compassion for them in that circumstance? Can you acknowledge that they are a fallible human being, susceptible to making mistakes? You don't need to justify or approve of what they did. But can you forgive them?

4. Forgive them.

5. On another day, pick another person you need to forgive. Work through the process in questions 2-4. Forgive them.

6. Repeat this process until you've forgiven every person on your list.

Chapter 11

Giving

The joys and benefits of giving are plentiful. How delightful it is to "pay forward" gifts received. Or to bestow kindnesses to strangers. How rewarding to give important people in your life special presents. How soul-affirming to contribute to the greater community.

Research in the field of Positive Psychology overwhelmingly confirms what you probably know from your own experience: Giving feels good and begets good.

Ж

Here's the next of *50 Ways to Enjoy Turning Fifty:*

Way #44: Commit random acts of kindness

During your fiftieth year, look for opportunities to give kindnesses to strangers. Let the frazzled mom go ahead of you at the checkout. Serve the lawn care people some cold melon on a hot day. Hand homeless people sandwiches or bottles of water. Every giving act makes the world a better place.

For goodness' sake, aim to commit acts of kindness during your milestone year.

ACTIVITY:

During your fiftieth year, aim to commit at least fifty acts of kindness to strangers.

Here's the next of *50 Ways to Enjoy Turning Fifty*.

Way #45: Identify what you can give to important people in your life

---

Jason hosted the best birthday party I've attended. He insisted that he wanted no presents, no libations, and no contributions to the event. Instead, he made a point of providing everything for the party — and giving his guests gifts.

"I like giving," he explained. "Giving makes me happy. I'd much rather give than receive so letting me do that is the best birthday gift you can give me."

He makes a great point. It feels great to give to those we care about. If we can provide them with something we know they need or want, even better.

You no doubt give the important people in your life gratitude, affection, and plenty more. During your fiftieth year, why not give them something special — as a way of celebrating your milestone? It might be a letter that details why they are special to you. Maybe there's something you were planning to give them "someday." Why wait? Do it now. It could be a family heirloom or a hand-crafted object made with affection. Maybe you know they need a particular item or would love a specific service. Perhaps they just want to spend time with you.

Kelli flew her two best friends to a five star hotel in the Florida Keys for a long weekend. It was a treat for them — and for her. "We had a blast," she reported.

ACTIVITY:	
List the names of the people you care about most.	For each person, brainstorm possible gifts.
Circle the gift you think each person would like most. Give it to them this year.	

Here's the next of *50 Ways to Enjoy Turning Fifty:*

Way #46: **Identify what you can offer your community**

Do you donate time or money to charity? Are there local populations needing volunteers? What services or talents can you offer in your community? What can you teach to others? Why not use your fiftieth to offer more of yourself?

Whatever your interests, there are ample options for you to contribute. Volunteer opportunities are easily found here: http://www.VolunteerMatch.org/

If you'd like to donate financially, ensure you are giving to organizations that are well-run, fiscally responsible, and do what they purport to do. Charity Navigator (https://www.CharityNavigator.org/) provides free, objective assessments of charities' financial health, accountability, and transparency.

Marsha volunteers in classrooms. Steve visits lonely seniors once a week. Pat helps out at the local animal shelter. John volunteers as a docent at a museum. Kevin mentors would-be entrepreneurs.

KEY QUESTIONS:

1. What talents do you have that would benefit your community?

2. What time or money or services could you offer?

3. What would be interesting for you to teach? To whom?

Chapter 12

Looking Forward

Turning fifty provides a natural opportunity to contemplate the legacy we're leaving behind. It's not just our descendants, if any — it's our net contribution to the world.

ЖК

Here's the next of *50 Ways to Enjoy Turning Fifty:*

Way #47: Think about your legacy

As long as we are we're giving more to the world than we're taking, that's a legacy. It's a matter of being responsible members of society, rather than harming others. Of being good stewards of the environment, rather than plundering it.

We can leave a legacy by:

- **growing and creating things, rather than just consuming**

Whether it's a vegetable garden or a handmade sweater, making things is a contribution.

Tracy believes her legacy lies in "upcycling" — in taking apparent trash and making something useful or beautiful with it.

- **loving more than hating**

As discussed in Chapter Ten, there are some people who are challenging to love — especially those who hurt us — and there are benefits to forgiving them (as we would want to be forgiven). Happily, it's easy to give affection to people we *do* care about. To truly appreciate them and what they bring to our lives. If you are turning fifty, you may be familiar with the lyrics of James Taylor: "Shower the people you love with love."

During his fiftieth year, Robert made a point of writing letters to express his affection for each person he deeply cared about.

- **sharing knowledge and ideas**

The more knowledge we can spread in our communities, our professions, and our personal lives, the greater the gift to the world.

People with ample resources set up foundations committed to particular causes. Others write books or create research or artworks or buildings or goods that enrich the world. Pat is devoted to promoting different animal welfare issues. Allison's mission is to free and exonerate people who have been wrongfully incarcerated. What is your preferred legacy?

KEY QUESTION:

Clear some uninterrupted time to contemplate your legacy.

1. What would you like to be your net contribution to the planet?

2. This is a morbid activity, but if you're comfortable trying it, it can be revealing:

(a) If you died today, what would your obituary say?

(b) Now imagine your preferred obituary. For what do you want to be remembered, say, twenty years after your death?

3. What actions can you take during your fiftieth towards your preferred legacy?

Here's the next of *50 Ways to Enjoy Turning Fifty:*

Way #48: **Contemplate the next decade of your life and how you'd like to live it**

Fifty is a pivot point to the rest of our lives. We can reflect, regroup, and choose the direction for our next chapter. We can do whatever we wish with this next decade.

What would **you** like to do with your fifties?

THOUGHT EXPERIMENT:

1. Clear some uninterrupted time. Imagine it's the eve of your sixtieth birthday. You are pleased and proud of your life. What's your life like? Be as detailed as possible. What's happened over the previous ten years? What have you done? What have you experienced? What have you learned or explored? What have you accomplished, acquired, or completed? Consider different aspects of your life:

- career / professional / financial

- family / domestic

- social

- learning / education / personal development

- health / fitness

- leisure activities / hobbies / long-term interests

- life dreams

---

2. Describe your "ideal" fifties. What's the life you'd love to live during the next ten years? How do you want to spend it? Where will you be? With whom? Be as detailed as possible.

3. Think about your current life, relative to your ideal.

- What's already in place? What's working well?

- What brings you joy? What brings you fulfilment?

- What would you like to do more of?

- What would you like to do less of? What would you like to reduce or eliminate from your life?

4. Review your lists on pages 119 and 120. Circle any items that jump out at you as being the most important, the most fun, or the most interesting things you'd really, truly love to have in your life.

5. Devise ways to make it happen. *For example if you're yearning to spend more time in nature, figure out a way to do so at least once a week. If you're hankering to learn to play guitar, sign up for a class, ask someone for lessons or download an app to teach yourself.*
What can you do to live the next decade as you would like?

Here's the next of *50 Ways to Enjoy Turning Fifty:*

Way #49: **Review your fiftieth year**

As you conclude your fiftieth year, take some time to reflect back on it. What's happened? How has the milestone been for you?

ACTIVITY:

At the conclusion of your fiftieth year, read through your notes in this book.

How have you been chronicling this milestone? Flip through your calendar entries, photos, scrapbook, etc. to remind yourself of your activities over the past twelve months. Read the contents of your Milestone Memory Bank (page 38).

KEY QUESTIONS:

Clear some uninterrupted time to think about your milestone year. Answer the following questions:

1. What's worked well?

2. What hasn't?

3. What have you enjoyed most?

4. What have you learned?

5. What has surprised you?

Here's the last of *50 Ways to Enjoy Turning Fifty:*

Way #50: Devise a plan to make 51 even better

Based on your review of your fiftieth year, you can devise ways to make the next year even better.

Debra did so well with her weight loss goals during her fiftieth year that she dedicated her fifty-first to working towards running a half-marathon. James exceeded the business goals he set out for himself for his fiftieth year…and decided to dedicate his next year to devising regular getaways with his family. My fifty frolics were so much fun, I've made it a yearly practice. (But each year I aim for one more…"51 Frolics", "52 Frolics"…etc.)

Let's be honest: Age ain't nothin' but a number. The purpose of this book has been to invite you to use turning fifty as an opportunity to do whatever is important to you…yet that number is kinda arbitrary. It's possible to apply any of the "50 Ways" to any (or every) year of your life.

Why not start with next year?

ACTIVITY:

1. As fast as you can, write down activities you'd like to do during your fifty-first year.

2. Think about a theme for your year. (E.g., fun, relaxation, learning, philanthropy, or whatever else.) Brainstorm theme-related activities you'd like to do next year.

---

3. Review the "50 Ways" listed in the Contents at the beginning of the book. Which are most appealing for you to do during your fifty-first year?

4. Think about the following areas of life. For each, jot down relevant activities you'd like to do during your fifty-first year. In each category, what do you want to do, honor, or explore this year? With whom? Where or how?

- career / professional / financial

- family / domestic

- social

- learning / education / personal development

- health / fitness

- leisure activities / hobbies / long-term interests

- life dreams

5. Pull out your planner and calendar. Plan your preferred fifty-first year.

Ж

Moving Forward

I wish you a Happy Fiftieth Birthday and a terrific fiftieth year. Make the most of it! I'd love to hear about it: Your stories, feedback, and suggestions for improvement on this book are most welcome. Please contact me here: **bit.ly/contactliisakyle**

This is also the best way to reach me if you'd like personalized help in making real, directed personal changes in your life.

If you'd like to receive free weekly email prompts to foster your personal development, please sign up here: **bit.ly/weeklyprompts**

Wishing you all the best,

Liisa Kyle, Ph.D.

Ж

Acknowledgements:

Sincere thanks to everyone who shared their stories and ideas for inclusion in this book.

Special thanks to Andy Bartels for reading an earlier draft and for his thoughtful, detailed suggestions for improvement.

About the Author

Liisa Kyle, Ph.D. is the go-to coach for smart, creative people who want to overcome challenges, get organized, get things done, and get more out of life. She's coached individuals, facilitated groups, and delivered inventive workshops on four continents. (www.LiisaKyle.com, www.CoachingForCreativePeople.com)

She's also an internationally published writer/editor/ photographer. She's authored books about

- happiness
- getting things done
- goal-setting and planning
- self-worth
- overcoming procrastination
- overcoming perfectionism
- getting over regrets, disappointments and past mistakes
- how to make the most of a milestone birthday, and
- how to make real, directed, personal change.

She earned her Ph.D. in Psychology from the University of Michigan.

Liisa Kyle co-founded The DaVinci Dilemma™ — an online community devoted to helping smart, creative people juggling too many talents, too many projects, and too many ideas. Check out her free self-help articles at www.DavinciDilemma.com.

She lives in the Pacific Northwest with her multi-talented spouse, a snuggly Yellow Lab, and a Labradoodle who looks like a *Dr. Seuss* character.

Contact: bit.ly/contactliisakyle

Free Weekly E-Mail Self-Coaching Prompts: bit.ly/weeklyprompts

Coaching Special Offers: bit.ly/LKspecialoffer

Books by Liisa Kyle, Ph.D.

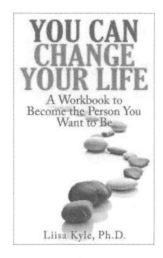

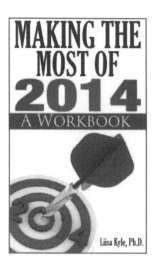

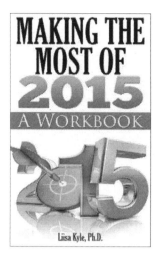

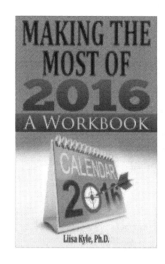

xx

Notes and Ideas for Enjoying My Fiftieth Year

Notes and Ideas for Enjoying My Fiftieth Year

67209438R00078

Made in the USA
Lexington, KY
05 September 2017